The Art of Illumination

RESIDENTIAL LIGHTING DESIGN

The Art of Illumination

RESIDENTIAL LIGHTING DESIGN

Glenn M. Johnson

I.A.L.D., I.E.S.N.A.

McGraw-Hill

New York   San Francisco   Washington, D.C.   Auckland   Bogotá
Caracas   Lisbon   London   Madrid   Mexico City   Milan
Montreal   New Delhi   San Juan   Singapore
Sydney   Tokyo   Toronto

McGraw-Hill

A Division of The **McGraw·Hill** *Companies*

1 2 3 4 5 6 7 8 9 0   9 0 3 2 1 0 9 8

ISBN 0-07-032958-3 (HC)
ISBN 0-07-032959-1 (PBK)

The sponsoring editor for this book was Wendy Lochner.

Printed in Hong Kong

NOTICE

This book is designed as a resource to those interested in residential lighting. Unless otherwise indicated, the lighting designs, and practices and procedures are the sole property of Glenn M. Johnson. The term "ADAPTIVE METHOD" is a trademark protected under federal and state law. Any commercial use of the term, the process or the good will associated with it is strictly prohibited without prior written permission from the author. Your cooperation is appreciated.

DEDICATION

I would like to dedicate this book to my family. To my father, Merlin E. Johnson, for assisting me in developing the gift of working with light. To my brothers, Duane and Eric, for the early learning times and experiences in San Francisco together, which could fill the pages of another book. To my mother, Peggy, for her support, compassion and patience in putting up with years of holiday gatherings, reunions and phone conversations ultimately revolving around lighting. And most importantly, to my beautiful wife, Charlene, and our five wonderful children Christopher, Scott, Matthew, Carly and Sarah. I love you all very much!

CONTENTS

FOREWORD

When most people think of residential lighting, they immediately gravitate towards traditional lighting decoration. Every competent interior designer learns how to select the "right" chandeliers and table lamps. Likewise, top residential architects select lighting fixtures for their appearance in a catalog, where the fixture is probably lighted by the photographer rather than by itself. The luminaires are selected as sculpture or ornament, consistent with the style and value of the home. A modest condominium apartment receives a nondescript $100.00 chandelier in the dining room; a $750,000.00 spec home gets a $2,500 crystal chandelier in the same spot. Both get a $2.99 dimmer. In both cases, the homeowner dims the lights and uses candles to create the proper mood. So much for "lighting design".

It was the odd marriage of electrical engineering and theatrical lighting that created professional lighting designers. Engineers are function and foot-candle oriented, and tend to design efficient lighting systems that meet building codes. Theatrical designers are appearance and mood oriented, and tend to design attractive spaces with drama and the right "mood". The professional lighting designer resolves these left-and right-brained challenges. Perhaps this is the appeal of the profession; very few challenge both sides of the brain so completely.

Residential lighting is the stepchild of professional lighting design. Until the late 1980's, almost every significant book about lighting design involved offices, stores, hotels, or theater lighting. Like architects, significant lighting designers undertook residential work reluctantly. I can't tell you how many times I have heard colleagues complain about doing homes. Too many changes, they'd say. Interior designers don't understand good lighting design. Owners won't pay for good lighting. I can't make money doing this kind of work. Takes too much hand-holding. And so on.

So you can imagine my surprise when I joined Fran Kellogg Smith at Luminae Lighting Consultants in San Francisco and discovered that, in California there was a rapidly growing desire for good residential lighting.

Ground breaking designs by the pioneers, notably Smith and David Winfield Wilson, caught the public eye. Interiors featuring lighting, especially low-voltage, by the California Five (Gaylord, Taylor, and company) were widely published. In turn, a new generation of interior designers (especially Alan Lucas and Charles Falls, who won several ASID/Halo design awards) and lighting designers (Jan Moyer, Nancy McCoy, Michael Souter and Randall Whitehead) promoted the state of the art to new levels. My firm Luminae Souter, grew out of this and enjoyed great success.

Take a look at the products whose importance in residential lighting is so prominent today. MR-16 lamps. Architectural fixture companies like Halo. Capri, Juno, and Lightolier. Specialty lighting companies like Lucifer, Boyd, Artemide and CSL. Dimming systems by Lutron, Lightolier, Vantage and Lite-touch. The golden days of evolution of lighting design in California have created a new standard of residential design combining traditional decorative values with the drama of lighting design.

During those years, Glenn M. Johnson emerged as the top designer in Los Angeles, Beverly Hills and the greater LA metro area. He grew up in Northern California in a family who still works in the lighting industry. Glenn was real smart—he understood the direct correlation between disposable income and lighting's dramatic potential—and staked out the most expensive real estate market in the continental U.S. He moved out of Southern California during the only recession there since the Ice Age—and quickly established himself as the preeminent residential lighting designer in the Rocky Mountain region. Glenn continues to work around the world, however, due to the quality of his work and his good name in the industry.

This book marks an important step in teaching lighting design. For most of the history of electric light, design education has been prescriptive. "Do this, it will work." The nation's utility companies, in a slower kinder era, offered free advice and in some cases, lighting showrooms for customers. General Electric heavily promoted residential lighting: many pre-1970 homeowners and interior designers learned what little we could teach them through GE publications or a trip to the Lighting Center at Nela. In the 1980's the residential torch was carried by Halo (through their affiliation with ASID) and Lightolier (through their dealer-based "lighting labs"). Serious books by Fran Kellogg Smith and Fred Bertolone, Jane Grosslight, and Randall Whitehead, and awareness books by Sunset and Ortho helped promote the opportunities. But still, something was missing. . . .

Last fall I reviewed Glenn's first manuscript and sent it back a with a number of recommendations. I really felt that this book is a breakthrough in teaching lighting design and I wanted to see it made as good as possible. The best part of this book for me is the clarity with which Glenn has identified the "layering" process of lighting design. By breaking lighting down into its various "duties" and then choosing a combination of luminaires to achieve the design requirements, Glenn has expressed what a every good lighting designer does.

The other thing that I love about Glenn's book is the context. Glenn is a designer not an academic or manufacturer. He does what he is writing about for a living and he does it well. Designers are often criticized for not sharing, but in Glenn's case, he opens up his mind and heart to many problems of residential lighting. His comments on team building are so important, I suggested he make a separate flyer about this. If he writes about it, it really happens and needs to be addressed.

Because I have been through it all and practice myself most of what Glenn has to say, I would suggest this book is interesting but will not change the way I work or the way the other 100 or so professional residential lighting designers in the U.S. work. But for the other 100,000 people who try to design lighting for a custom home every year, this book is essential reading. I recommend it highly to the architects, interior designers, contractors, developers, builders, lighting showroom sales people and lighting distributors who do this kind of work. Combine this book with Randall Whitehead's *Residential Lighting*, a coffee table picture book with this caliber of lighting , and one could easily understand the greatest compliment to Glenn's book is that he has risked telling his readers the "secret" of residential lighting such that every one who reads it becomes his (and my) competition. Our only real advantage is that we have 20 years' (or more) experience, and you, the reader, are just learning.

James Robert Benya, PE,FIES,IALD,LC
Principal
Pacific Lightworks LLC
Portland, OR USA and
Pacific Lightworks Canada Ltd
Vancouver, BC Canada
January 14, 1998

ACKNOWLEDGMENTS

The author credits numerous individuals for the production of this work. For their generous time and making themselves available he extends appreciation to Kari L. Mitchell for her editing skills and sharing 4 years as an Associate Lighting Designer and assistant to the author; to Andrew M. Mitchell for his wonderful eye in preserving the integrity of the author's illuminated spaces through his photography; to Todd C. Bello for his computer skills in preparing graphics, imaging and related expertise; to Greg H. Hurst and Mike L. Larsen, Associate Lighting Designer for their computer drafting expertise; and to Ellen J. Clubb, Kris L. Wilde, Associate Lighting Designer, and Bradley A. Bouch, Associate Lighting Designer for review and support in the final preparations of the manuscript. Also thanks to Digital Interiors, Inc. of San Jose, Ca.; Skip Marsh and Steve Raschke for their input and insight with Chapter 19 "Home Trends."

INTRODUCTION

In practicing lighting design for the past 20 plus years for the custom residential market, I realized that a book of this magnitude was critical to the forward progress of the industry. Lighting design is one of the most exciting elements in homes today and it is equally rewarding when the client can witness and experience the fruits of the lighting designer's labors. Myself and others involved in this exclusive industry have largely been educators due to the fact that there was no forum. It has been our responsibility to inform the architects, interior designers and ultimately the homeowners of the benefits of a well planned lighting system. The difficult part of our industry is that there is very little (or no) training, schooling, publications or other means that specifically focus on residential lighting design. So, without a program in place or a manual to refer to, I realized I should bring this exciting, rewarding practice to the forefront.

My training and experience:
In my early years of electrical and lighting apprenticeship, I worked side by side with my mentor/ father, Merlin E. Johnson of Artistic Lighting, an unsung hero who is a true pioneer in the field of lighting design, and my brothers, Duane and Eric. Merlin taught that if a lighting fixture or application for a specific task was not yet explored through current manufacturers or practices, then design it yourself. Even though the common lamps and lighting products used in the early 1970s were quite simple in nature, Merlin designed complex lighting systems for specific tasks that needed to be integrated into the home. Under his direction we would modify available products or make our own which incorporated specialty lamps that would fill the need and then install them into the home.

One example of this type of modification would be: for artwork illumination in the 1970's, lamp sources were limited for accenting paintings. We only had the common A lamp (the standard household lamp) and the R lamp (reflector lamp) which was only available in a spot and a flood. Our task was to artistically and dramatically illuminate a fine painting at a reasonable cost with a small, unobtrusive aperture in the ceiling. Merlin directed us to investigate the 12 volt 1157 lamp source (the automobile tail light lamp) and come up with an enclosed housing with adjustable trim for the application. By utilizing low-voltage sources for accent lighting, we were way ahead of the industry, as it would be more than a decade before the introduction of the MR16 and MR11 halogen lamps.

This early training has allowed me to look beyond the existing products and focus on the task at hand. I currently have 3 U.S. patents on specialty lighting products and have designed over 10 lighting products on the market today. I did this not because I am a fixture designer, but because I looked first at the task at hand and could not find an existing product that would perform that task. (Note: today, it is critical for safety and liability purposes that any designs and/or modifications are completed by a professional lighting manufacturer with approval of U.L. (Underwriters Laboratories) or other equivalent testing agencies.) It is my hope that this approach encourages other residential lighting designers to explore their own ideas with the emphasis on creativity.

One of the weakest links in residential lighting design has been in the drawings and documentation side of the practice. The lighting design is only as good as it is communicated and I have always felt that the documents should stand on their own. After I or my staff leave the project's site, the professionalism should carry on with precise, easy to understand maps and guidelines for execution by the general and electrical contractor. Residential lighting design has been my life. I have been fortunate to have had the opportunity to witness and assist in the progress (from this infantile stage) of my profession.

NOTE →

Over the years I have illuminated some of the nation's most exclusive homes for a clientele list that reads as the Who's Who of the arts, entertainment and business world. I have been very serious about this profession and hope that my experience and practical approach to illuminating homes becomes an industry standard or at least a springboard for forward progress. I would encourage any student interested in architecture, interior design or other related professions to consider lighting design as an occupation. Universities are now offering courses of study in lighting design and manufacturers of lighting fixtures and lamps offer training seminars on their products and use. Professional organizations such as the American Institute of Architects (AIA) the American Society of Interior Designers (ASID), and Consumer Electronics Design and Installation Association (C.E.D.I.A.) offer courses on lighting taught

NOTE →

by lighting professionals. Please take advantage of these resources and others like them. Remember that you can have the ability to create a remarkable home environment through artistic lighting design. Do not be satisfied with anything less.

For the consumer who is looking to retain a lighting designer to add the necessary drama and excitement to their home, it is critical to do the research! Add these professionals to your project's team. Look on the Internet under residential lighting design, call for references from such prestigious lighting designs organizations as Illumination Engineering Society of North America (I.E.S.N.A.) and the International Association of Lighting Designers (I.A.L.D.).

This book has been a dream of mine for several years. I have been fortunate in my career to have experienced working with talented architects, interior designers and builders who have taught me over the years their practices. It is now time to reciprocate and share with the design and building community what I have learned.

In order for us to receive anything with gratitude we must truly experience the joy of giving.

GLENN M. JOHNSON

Part 1

The Elements of Residential Lighting Design

CHAPTER ONE

What is a Lighting Designer?

New technologies always require a specialist. Technology has increasingly become the driving force in the world of home building and design. Lighting design is one profession that has escalated in growth over the past few years due to this trend. An experienced lighting designer creates an atmosphere that is warm, inviting, subtle and artistic through proper placement, selection and control of various lighting products. Seasoned lighting designers come from various design disciplines and trades, including, theatrical and engineering backgrounds. It has only been during the last decade that accredited lighting design programs were offered on the university level. Currently, Penn State, University of Colorado, Rensselaer, Parsons and other institutions offer such courses. Literature regarding university programs in lighting design is available through I.E.S.N.A. (see resource appendix) ~~Pop~~ *Poly technical school*

In most cases, the professional residential lighting designer is different than the commercial lighting designer, just as the residential architect and interior designer differ from their commercial counterparts. The reasons for specialization are evident due to the following areas: electrical codes; lighting fixtures; dimming controls; lamp types and use; maintenance issues; and, practices and procedures. Based on the vast differences mentioned above, most professional lighting design practices have separate residential and commercial design departments (the latter being the most prevalent in the industry).

The lighting design industry is still in its early stages and subsequently the process of searching out and selecting a seasoned design professional is a little difficult. There are two main organizations that aid in this process by defining the lighting design industry and the practice of a lighting designer: the Illuminating Engineering Society of North America (I.E.S.N.A.); and, the International Association of Lighting Designers (I.A.L.D.). Both of these organizations set high standards for the industry and offer critical guidelines which address safety, energy, aesthetics and business ethics. The professional lighting designer is, in most cases, a member of one or both of these prestigious organizations.

- **I.E.S.N.A.** Established in 1906, this organization welcomes all within the lighting industry: manufacturers, product representatives, educators, engineers and designers (current membership is approximately 9,000 members). This group is heavily involved in education and standards writing. The organization is broken into national, regional, local and student chapters. The local sections often present two instructional programs each year and educate thousands of participants. Every five years, I.E.S.N.A. issues a standards manual, which is considered to be <u>the</u> authoritative guide on lighting applications and technology. Other I.E.S.N.A. publications provide additional information on more specialized fields, such as illuminating sports arenas, casinos, theaters and shopping malls. The organization provides ongoing educational articles in their monthly publication <u>LD+A</u>. Membership is open to anyone with an interest in lighting and who meets established requirements.

I.A.L.D. Founded in 1969, this international organization is open to professional lighting consultants who design lighting plans and specify fixtures, but do not supply product. Strict membership requirements involving the designer's conduct, practice, skill and expertise must be met by the applicant. The organization promotes the benefits of hiring a professional lighting designer and has several educational opportunities for designers throughout the year. The largest annual event co-sponsored by I.A.L.D. is LIGHTFAIR International, where informative seminars and new product demonstrations further the designers' knowledge. I.A.L.D. offers a grant/scholarship program that exposes students to the career opportunities of lighting design.

Although membership in one or both of the above organizations indicates professional status, certification of lighting designers is being encouraged throughout the industry. The National Council on Qualifications for the Lighting Professions (N.C.Q.L.P.) is a non-profit organization that has established certification requirements for lighting professionals. Founded in 1992, N.C.Q.L.P. has organized an examination for professionals to demonstrate their knowledge and experience in the various facets of lighting design. The credential "LC", Lighting Certified, is given to those who have passed this test. Testing began in November 1997, and will support the widespread recognition of this professional credential.

In selecting a lighting designer, the client must realize that the practice of residential lighting design combines several disciplines. The lighting designer must: *Budget*
- be sensitive to the clients' needs.
- be able to evaluate and accommodate the architectural designs of a given building.
- have strong construction knowledge in order to communicate effectively with the construction team.
- be experienced in interior design in order to enhance the other design aspects.
- be a team player.
- be an expert in the capabilities of lighting fixtures and lamps.
- be an expert in lighting control systems, from the simplest wall box dimmer to sophisticated micro-processor based systems.
- have electrical contracting and engineering experience to design lighting systems consistent with local and national building codes.
- present lighting equipment and prices for budgeting purposes.
- not be in the supply business, thus avoiding any conflict of interest.

Programming ✓✓ - talk to client

- ultimately design an aesthetically pleasing environment without the distraction of unsightly glare and overbearing lighting products.

The following are services that should be provided by a professional lighting designer:
- team coordination with all design and construction disciplines .
- full architecturally related drawings including, but not limited to: floor plans, reflected ceiling plans, sections, details, pertinent elevations and lighting equipment placement.
- lighting control system design and coordination.
- lighting fixture specification and budgets.
- attendance at design meetings.
- construction review of lighting installation.
- lighting adjustments during construction and move-in phases.

Additional criteria for selecting a lighting designer include: evaluation of the designer's performance; experience; knowledge; artistic ability; engineering; construction skills; fee structure; and, compatibility.

Evaluating Performance
The lighting designer should provide a reference list of clients, architects and interior designers. The potential client should speak with the general contractors and electrical contractors associated with past projects to determine if the lighting designer's work and services were performed in a professional and organized manner.

Evaluating Experience
The clients need to review the lighting designer's portfolio. The lighting designer who does not have a portfolio prepared for presentation is operating at a disadvantage. A portfolio of past work is critical for all design professionals. The clients should evaluate the quality and versatility of the work displayed in the portfolio content.

Evaluating Knowledge
The clients should research the prospective lighting designer's education and work experience. Is he or she a salesperson from the local lighting showroom or a manufacturer's representative? Does the lighting designer have experience in relevant fields such as theater lighting design, electrical engineering, electrical contracting, interior design and architecture? If the designer is new to the field, research their level of educational training and practical experience.

Evaluating Fee Structure
Professional fees are commonly based on the designer's skill level and experience. Most lighting designers establish the fee on a square footage basis, as a percentage of the overall construction costs, or charge per hour. An associate lighting designer may be billed out as little as $65.00/hour, while a principal designer may charge as much as $200.00/hour. In order to avoid unexpected surprises, it is advisable to find a designer who charges on a square footage basis with the scope of services predetermined at the outset of the project.

Evaluating Compatibility

After extensive research and a portfolio presentation, the clients should be able to determine the designer's compatibility with the rest of the design team. The team concept is based on flexibility and cooperation between team members – negative egos do not survive in this type of process.

THE FUTURE OF THE PROFESSION

In the near future, professional residential lighting designers will automatically be retained for a project. This is the current procedure for the commercial lighting design industry. Hopefully, the basis for employment will be different, as most commercial lighting designers are initially hired because of liability issues. Injuries sustained in a commercial building (from a fall or other such accident) incur high liability damages. Lawyers filing a legal suit will name everyone involved in the commercial building — the architect, contractor, interior designer, lighting designer, and the remainder of the staff. The commercial lighting designer has a tremendous responsibility in ensuring that all areas of building lighting meet the recommended standards and practices of the Illuminating Engineering Society (I.E.S.N.A.). This society has set the recommended practices for public and task locations of commercial buildings. The lighting designer will be held responsible if specified lighting levels are not met and someone is injured in the building. In fact, one of the insurance investigator's most utilized tools is a light meter and it is used to measure and catalog the illumination levels of a given space.

Conversely, residential lighting design does not have the same legal concerns because the home is not usually occupied by large groups of people. Residential lighting designers can be more creative without the stress of foot-candle measurements. They look first at the artistic side of illumination rather than lumen calculations. The creative aspect of residential lighting design should be a professional priority, rather than an afterthought. The team approach to home design and building will also continue to improve the professional future of residential lighting design. That future will necessitate a residential lighting design organization with its own standards and practices. Educational seminars on residential lighting design will continue to be offered to professional organizations, such as the American Institute of Architects (A.I.A.), the American Society of Interior Designers (A.S.I.D), the Consumer Electronics Design and Installation Association (C.E.D.I.A.), the National Association of Home Builders (N.A.H.B.), the Designers Lighting Forum (D.L.F.), the American Lighting Association (A.L.A.), and others (see Resource Appendix).

The number of professional residential lighting designers will increase along with the enhanced level of available training and information. Continual growth in the industry will lead to strict testing and licensing standards. As of this writing, both the residential and commercial lighting design fields can practice without licensing or regulation.

CHAPTER TWO

The History and Future of Residential Lighting Design

Figure 2.1
Residence with traditional
* lighting.*
(Photographer: Mary E. Nichols)

THE HISTORY OF RESIDENTIAL LIGHTING DESIGN

Until the late 1940's, the requirements of illuminating a home, even a mansion, were quite simple. Lighting design consisted of installing switches and a few wall outlets for plug-in decorative lamps – plus, adding wall sconces and surface or pendant center ceiling fixtures in most rooms. The design was commonly performed by the electrician, who would walk the room in the framing stage with an 8 foot stick. The stick had several heights marked on it: one at 12 inches locating the wall outlets; one at 42 inches locating the switches; and a third, at 72 inches locating the wall sconces. The electrician would also take the stick and swing it from the four corners of the room to locate the center ceiling outlet for the chandelier or other surface mounted fixture.

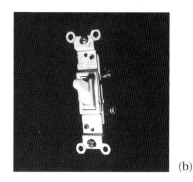

(a)

(b)

Figure 2.2
(a) A and candelabra lamp.
(b) Toggle switch.
(c) Push button switch.
(Photographer: Andrew M.
Mitchell, FPI)

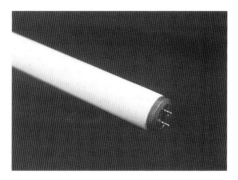

(c)

The typical light sources were the incandescent A lamp, and the Candelabra lamp controlled by a toggle or push button switch.

A number of homes adopted fluorescent lamps about 1942.

Figure 2.3
Fluorescent tube.
(Photographer: Andrew M.
Mitchell, FPI)

Fluorescent lamps produced much more raw illumination for less energy than the incandescent A lamp. However, their poor color rendition, awkward size, and slight flicker kept the lamps out of wide residential use until product improvements were made.

A new level of sophistication was introduced into the lighting industry in the 1940s with the advent of the reflector or "R" lamp.

The R lamp was designed to project light rather than radiate it in all directions (like the standard A lamp). The process was completed through the use of a reflective coating applied to the inside of the back portion of the lamp. This exciting new lamp later triggered the broad use of the recessed downlight fixture which was originally intended for illuminating houses of worship from the

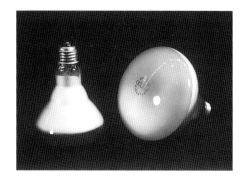

Figure 2.4
Reflector lamp.
(Photographer: Andrew M.
Mitchell, FPI)

high ceilings. The projected light allowed the congregation to read their hymnals, as well as find the collection basket. Consumers could now use these new recessed cans in their residences. The lights were flush with the ceiling, provided for area and wall wash lighting, and offered an alternative to decorative wall sconces, chandeliers and decorative lamps for illumination. With this new fixture, everyone became lighting designers as they added rows upon rows of recessed lights to interior spaces (often using a grid pattern). The ceilings became pocked with black holes and unfortunately detracted from the architectural and interior features of the home.

Figure 2.5
Grid illumination.

The track light was the next fixture to utilize the R and A lamps when it gained popularity in the early 1960s. Track lights were employed when recessed joist space did not allow for the newly developed large recessed cans. The R lamp was still large (5 inch diameter), which meant the track head or lamp holder needed to be even bigger in order to house the lamp. These large fixtures projected from the ceiling, and once again architecture took a back seat to innovation.

Figure 2.6
Track lighting.

Even though these were exciting developments, the focus was on the lighting products, not their performance and efficiency in the setting. Although technology has made tremendous strides since this time, track lights and recessed cans function as easy tools and are still utilized in vast quantities in today's production of model homes, custom homes, and even estate residences.

Dimmers were used to subdue the excessive illumination as spaces became over lit by recessed-down lights and track lights. Dimmers added a new dimension to lighting by allowing homeowners to create mood and drama.

Figure 2.7
Left: Rotary dimmer.
(Photographer:
Andrew M. Mitchell, FPI)

Figure 2.8
Right: Multiple dimmers
result in wall clutter.
(Photographer:
Joseph M. Good, III)

The standard wall dimmer at the time was only rated for a 600 watt incandescent load and resulted in wall clutter (multiple dimmers ganged in numerous locations throughout the home).

In the late 1970s, new lamp technology was introduced in the United States by General Electric. The 12 volt halogen lamp, originally designed for slide projectors, was the object of an experiment by lighting designer Ron Mendaleski. Ron was not satisfied with the lighting products available on the American market, so he turned to the new low voltage technology and created innovative lighting products. He was the first lighting designer/manufacturer to develop a miniature set of recessed-down lights and miniature track fixtures to house the new 12 volt MR16 and subsequent MR11 (multi-reflector) high intensity sources.

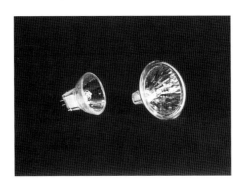

Figure 2.9
MR11 and MR16 lamps
(Photographer: Andrew M. Mitchell, FPI)

The introduction of the MR16 and MR11 lamps to the lighting industry provoked their consequent success with lighting designers around the country. Major lighting manufacturers slowly jumped on the bandwagon and started to develop limited varieties of low voltage recessed, surface-mounted, and track products. These products are often the main lighting sources in the home today.

In addition to these advances, vast improvements were made in lighting controls. Dimming technology developed in the 1960s, for the performing arts industry, was modified and refined to fit the residential lifestyle. This sophistication led to dimmers that could handle greater wattage in smaller packages and began the breakthrough research in computerized lighting and dimming control systems.

As the 21st century approaches, the field of lighting design continues to mature. Lighting fixtures are smaller and more functional. Energy efficiency and aesthetics have replaced grid illumination as leading concepts. The approach to lighting design has been refined to an art and science. No longer is it a common practice to just fill the room with light fixtures. Professional lighting designers specifically locate fixtures within the architecture to achieve dramatic and functional effects. New lighting technology has many possible uses in the residential industry.

Figure 2.10
(a) Fiber optic detail.
(b) Fiber optic lighting.
(Photographer:
Andrew M. Mitchell, FPI)

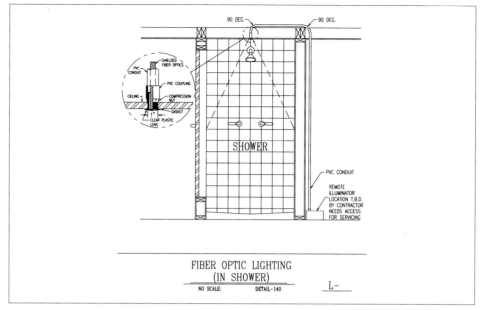

(a)

(b)

For example, fiber optics allow for unique applications because the lamp source can be located remotely within the structure. Difficult-to-light areas such as showers, saunas and pools can now be illuminated by 1-inch aperture end-lit, lensed fiber optic with no chance of electrical hazard in these wet locations.

New lamp technology has also exploded on the industry scene.

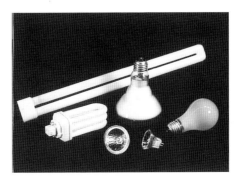

Figure 2.11
Over the years lamp selection
has grown.
(Photographer:
Andrew M. Mitchell, FPI)

Developments in fluorescent lamps have resulted in increased energy savings, better color rendering, dimming capabilities and smaller tube sizes. Compact fluorescent lamps are slowly replacing the standard A lamp. The R lamp, the workhorse of yesterday, has been labeled as an "energy hog". PAR lamps now last longer and use less energy. Low-voltage MR16 and MR11 fixtures are available in a wider range of wattage and beam spreads, along with an increased life span.

Lighting controls have developed into microprocessor-based systems.

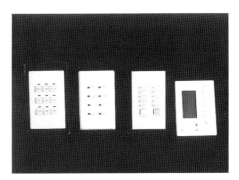

Figure 2.12
Microprocessor based lighting
controls.
(Photographer:
Andrew M. Mitchell, FPI)

The imagination is the only limiting factor to the vast possibilities in dimming and multiple switching. Designed properly, these systems allow for convenience, security, flexibility, energy savings and aesthetics. Through the use of small wall devices, these systems can compliment the decor and allow master switching of light groupings, dimming, dramatic scenes, pathway capabilities, and timed functions.

Increasing concern over energy use and misuse has prompted the government to pass legislation regarding lamp sources. For example, California's Title 24 sets guidelines on kitchen and bath lighting and stipulates that the primary lamp sources must have at least 40 lumens per watt. Currently, the only inexpensive luminaries to fulfill this criteria are fluorescent. The U.S. Department of Energy reports that residential households could save 31.7 billion kilowatt-hours of electricity annually if they replaced their most heavily used incandescent lamps with compact fluorescent lamps. This is enough electricity to light about one third of all U.S. households for an entire year (Energy Savings with Fluorescent Lighting Technology, EIA Reports, U.S. Department of Energy September 23, 1996).

Energy legislation targeted for commercial building illumination continues to have an impact on how residences are illuminated. On October 24, 1992 the Energy Policy Act (EPACT) was passed into law. Although many lamps were more efficient by this time, their initial cost was significantly higher than average. As a result, cheaper, less efficient sources like the R lamp were still being utilized by the mass market. To combat this tactic, EPACT restricted the use of certain inefficient lamps, like the R lamp and the larger T-12 fluorescent tubes. Consequently, lamp manufacturers like General Electric, Phillips, and Osram Sylvania have addressed this issue by replacing inefficient lamps in their product line.

The U.S. Environmental Protection Agency has developed a non-regulatory program aimed at promoting energy efficiency through lighting design and product selection. This program is called Energy Star. Energy Star states that a typical household spends about $110 dollars per year on lighting and most of it is wasted on inefficient light bulbs (lamps). It also points out that if everyone in the United States switched over to energy efficient Energy Star labeled fixtures and lamps that we could save 70 billion kilowatt-hours and prevent 100 billion pounds of carbon dioxide per year. (U.S. EPA ENERGY STAR Residential Lighting Fixture Program). Energy legislation and smart lighting design have improved the contemporary lifestyle and will positively contribute to the future.

The Future of Residential Lighting Design

Current technological advances continue to hint at future surprises for industry application. Global initiatives are currently accelerating on a record breaking track. Management of change will play an important part in the success of this burgeoning technology. Risk-taking and flexibility are key factors in assisting the evolution of these advances. History clearly documents the evolution of light emitting sources: fire; wax candles; kerosene lamps; natural gas lanterns; electric lamps; and, light guides, including fiber optics and light pipes with a single remote illumination source. The resulting progress, from numerous transitions in lighting history, has had a tremendous impact on living standards and quality of life. There is evidence to indicate this progress will continue to advanced levels of achievement. Lighting designers and lighting research centers are on the front line as they lead their industry and profession out of its infancy. Great strides in new electric lamp technology and other alternative energy saving products will support this progress and usher in the original promise of technology: a better way of life (see Resource Appendix).

Energy efficiency will continue to be the name of the game in residential lighting. In the not so distant future, the majority of homes' lighting will be produced by solar energy transmitted by fiber optic or other lighting guides that will direct the required lighting to the appropriate location. Solar energy will be kept in a type of storage device that will allow the transmission of light during the night, and storage replenishment during the day. Lighting control systems may consist of pneumatic wall switches or sensors that, when activated, will open the ends of the various light guides at the fiber optic hub and allow the transmission of light. Filters will be placed within the pneumatic mechanism that will vary the light levels for different intensities — low, medium and high. (the world's first air dimmer!). The cost of the system will include: the price of the fiber optic or other light guides; the filters; the air lines; the switches and sensors; the air compressor; the light guide hubs; and, the solar collector and storage device. The installation of the optical cabling will be done by a certified fiber optic technician who will be trained in running, splicing and terminating the optics into the illuminators and fittings. The best part is that the energy would be free as long as the sun remained in the sky. The only electric device for the lighting might be a back-up, high intensity light source that would charge the solar storage device in lieu of the sun. The role of the lighting designer at this juncture in history will be to design and engineer the optical cabling throughout the home and select the various adjustable and focusable irises. Actual linear footage of optic will be minimized by locating centralized rooms or equipment lockers on each floor of the house. Setting the lighting levels for optimum use and effects will be achieved through placement of the filters for desired results.

In order for this technology to become standard, the fiber optic industry must begin to find ways to lower the cost of the fiber optic itself. The initial product pricing is high, just like any new technology. As demand increases, so does competition between manufacturers, thus driving down the pricing that will allow fiber optic to become a main stream product. This market cycle has occurred repeatedly in product manufacturing processes.

The following quote on the future of residential lighting design is by

Joseph M. Good, III, LC, IESNA, IALD
President IESNA

Lighting becomes increasingly more complex each day. From prehistoric reliance on daylight and fire to today's newest sources and technology, progress is continuous and accelerating. The most significant and successful changes in the past three decades have been reactions to economic events or pressure. From the mid 1970's to mid 1980's lighting was examined and advanced from an energy consumption perspective, generally to reduce dependence on imported oil. Since the mid 1980's serious concern for the environment impact of fulfilling our insatiable need for electrical energy has created opportunities for "better" lighting. Both of these succeeded only as long as the short term economic analysis was favorable. External incentives, economic or statutory, were required to mitigate the pressure of first cost in favor of life cycle costs.

The future of lighting design and application will follow a similar model, with economic incentives driving most projects and innovations. Increasingly, two new differences will have an effect on the old paradigms. These are the increasing use of more complicated technology and the more difficult lighting challenges to accommodate the aging population. New technology in lamp, ballast, optics and control systems make the analysis and selection of lighting equipment more difficult than ever before. The choices are often bewildering. A professional will be invaluable in guiding consumers to the best product selections for each application. "One size fits all" solutions won't be satisfactory. Changes will come too fast for the casual practitioner to keep up.

Secondly, the U.S. population will have more senior citizens than teenagers by 2020. The challenges of lighting the visual environment for senior citizens are far more complicated than today's "lowest common denominator" lighting approaches.

The IESNA and IALD are working separately and together to modify the thinking in this area from simple illuminance "tables" (with weighting factors) to more comprehensive metrics that consider up to seven criteria before a lighting recommendation which will include illuminance, color, contrast, and/or other factors.

Continuing education in lighting will be necessary for designers, architects, sales forces, contractors, and consumers. Many government authorities and property owners will require that lighting be designed and maintained by certified and/or licensed persons. Today's solutions may be adapted to fit and work in tomorrow's world, but the best solutions will come from future technologies and imagination.

The following quote on the future of residential lighting design is by

Randy Burkett, IALD
IALD President 1996-1997

It has only been in the last decade that lighting design firmly established itself as a recognized discipline in the design field. Rapid advances in lighting technologies now and in the future have made the lighting designer nearly indispensable on mid to large scale projects. A more sophisticated end-user also understands the important role lighting can play in the success of a built environment and is demanding a suitable measure of expertise from the design team.

Presently, North America boasts the largest and most experienced pool of lighting designers in the world. However, it is in Europe, Asia and Australia where the biggest strides are being made. Traditionally, much of the lighting "design" in these areas has been done by the multi-national lighting manufacturers, in consultation with the project electrical engineers. As in North America, clients are elevating their expectations with regard to lighting and ask for creative, innovative design focus from independent, consultants. The profession is starting to blossom.

The future of the lighting design profession has never looked stronger. As clients' demands and expectations continue to grow, the lighting designer's role in the process will only become more vital to the project's overall success.

CHAPTER THREE:

Building a Custom Home —
Utilizing the Team Approach

Building a custom residence can be a demanding and time consuming process. With the assistance of an architect, homeowners decide on a wide variety of issues, from materials and finishes to the dwelling's square footage. Residential design and building have become more intricate and homeowners' choices have grown increasingly complex.

Figure 3.1
The construction of today's custom residence is becoming increasingly complex (Photographer: Andrew M. Mitchell, FPI)

Owners can be overwhelmed by the expanded use of lighting, audio/video, communication, computer, security, and home control systems. Experts in the various fields should be consulted, since the architect cannot be a specialist in every discipline.

When experts are organized into a team at the beginning of the design process, they help the owners make educated, timely and cost-effective decisions. As in professional sports, each team member has a specific task to perform in harmony with the other trained and experienced players. If there is no harmony, success can be stunted in the endeavor. Unfortunately, the team concept is new to the residential design and building process. A review of common practices in the building industry illustrates why the team approach is an important advancement.

Figure 3.2

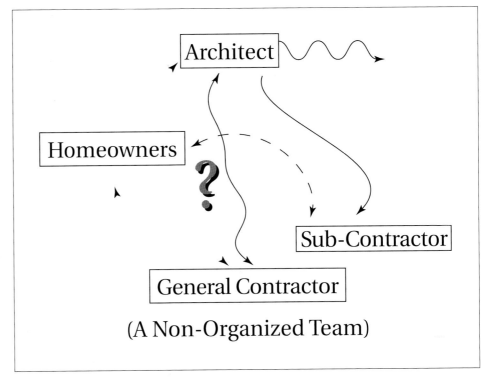

THE OLD PROCESS: NO ORGANIZED TEAM

In most cases, the architect designs a concept based on the homeowners' initial requirements. Architectural drawings are developed to present the collective elements in an organized, understandable manner, including floor plans, reflected ceiling plans, exterior elevations and a few interior building sections. Slight modifications become routine following the presentation of the plans: rooms are made larger or smaller; hallways are widened; windows are added or deleted; and, the exterior of the home is modified to match the owners' preconceived vision.

At this point, the architect and the homeowners begin to discuss construction budgets (based on the preliminary plans). These budget numbers are for the basic shell of the home and may include calculations to handle the <u>minimum</u> required plumbing, electrical, mechanical, and cabinetry. These estimated, baseline prices do not include any upgrades in lighting, electrical, low voltage infrastructure wiring, plumbing, tile, carpet, cabinets, and other materials. The owners are usually unaware of this minimal costing approach at this stage.

The next step is the architect's preparation of a set of plans and documents. These materials will be presented to the city for a building permit and to the bidding general contractors for a more accurate estimate of the construction costs. In order to complete this document set, the architect must add necessary lighting and electrical elements to the plan to obtain a permit from the building department.

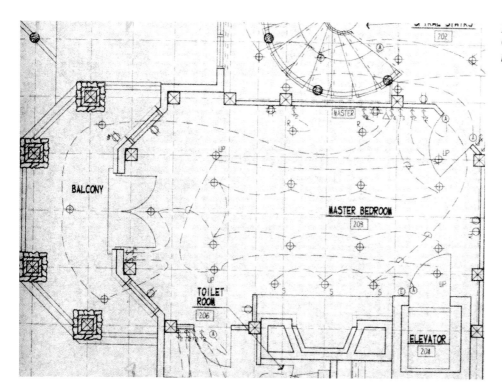

Figure 3.3
Generic lighting and electrical plan for building permit.

Unfortunately, these items are added at the last minute with very little planning and limited information on fixtures or equipment specifications.

In order to be cost-competitive with the other bidders, contractors must prepare pricing based solely on specific items in the architectural documents. General contractors know the plans are generic in nature, however they instruct their subcontractors (i.e., electrical, plumbing and mechanical contractors) to bid the plan <u>exactly</u> as it is designed by the architect. At this point, the bidding subcontractors have only minimal information as it relates to their field of expertise (as referenced in the architectural drawings and specifications). For example, a common practice in the residential architectural community is to represent lighting fixtures as circles on the plans. These symbols are designated as either recessed or surface mounted fixtures. There are no specific instructions as to product, manufacturer or tasks the fixtures are to perform in respective environments. In the absence of detailed information, the electrical contractor will select (by default) the least expensive products to ensure that the bid is competitive. Other bidding contractors make selections in exactly the same manner with insufficient information.

After receiving minimal bids, the general contractors combine the subcontractors' prices with their own and submit them to the homeowners. After reviewing compiled bids, the owners select a general contractor. More often than not, the building costs are higher than original expectations. The owners must decide whether to reduce the size of the residence or return to the lending institution for additional construction funds.

In the next phase, the general contractor usually requests a meeting with the architect and the homeowners to discuss the home's construction and determine what to do about unspecified items. The owners begin to realize how generic the plans are in relation to the lighting, lighting control, electrical elements, plumbing fixtures, cabinetry, tile, carpets, and other features that were not accurately bid due to the lack of definite specifications. Weary of the whole process, even before initial construction, the owners ask, "Who is responsible for supplying this detailed information?"

For the first time during the course of the project, the question of hiring specialized consultants is discussed by involved parties. Advice from experts can make the difference between a nice residence and a remarkable home. For example, a lighting designer may recommend specialty techniques that will make a home truly unique, such as: adding coves for indirect lighting, or accent lighting for artwork and furnishings. If consultants are retained as a resource, the subcontractors will finally have the detailed specifications and information they require to accurately re-bid and build the home.

In many cases, the step of considering consultants does not take place until building has begun on the project. Awareness of the importance of pre-planning usually arises once the walls are in place, the roof is on, and the windows are being installed at the site. In the case of lighting placement, this late approach is not cost effective and often ends in additional charges and change orders. The plumber and mechanical installers have already mapped installation in critical locations throughout the structure. Air-conditioning ducts or sprinkler lines positioned mid-hallway often need to be relocated to accommodate recessed lighting.

Figure 3.4
Ceiling coordination is critical to the correct placement of lighting fixtures. (Carm and Nancy Santoro Residence) (Photographer: Andrew M. Mitchell, FPI)

Lighting of this type aesthetically looks and performs better *centered* in the hallway space.

The owners may question the architect and general contractor as to who should pay consultants' fees and feel that the extra costs should be included in the architectural package. They may ask why the architect did not mention specialized consultants earlier in the process. In reality, the standard architectural contract only covers lighting and electrical plans sufficient enough to qualify for a building permit. It is not an architect's customary responsibility to determine that the initial drawings and documents have enough adequate information for the completion of the project.

The next step occurs once the owners agree to meet with various consultants who will round out the design process. Design issues in residential lighting illustrate how planning can affect results. A typical meeting with the lighting designer includes a professional portfolio presentation, during which the owners review beautiful photographs of interior and exterior lighting effects.

Figure 3.5
Lighting presentation to home-owners.
(Video clip by
Andrew M. Mitchell, FPI)

They evaluate testimonies of previous clients, builders, architects and interior designers which attest to the significant contribution made by professional lighting design. Lighting control systems are also discussed and presented at the meeting. The owners may meet with an audio/video specialist or other consultants, as they further define the desired elements for their home.

The process of randomly hiring consultants as needed may seem to go smoothly until one specialist requires information from another (who has yet to be retained). For example, the lighting designer needs a furniture layout, interior sections, reflected ceiling plans, detailed wall, ceiling and cabinetry information, as well as flooring and wall material selections to begin work on the lighting plans. Again, these items are outside of the architect's standard agreement. Preliminary lighting plans will be delayed and will include plenty of guesswork if an interior designer is not retained at the beginning of the process. An increased burden is placed upon the homeowners to assist with keeping the project on schedule — and they are called on to promptly deliver necessary information to the consultants.

The owners feel a great deal of discomfort and confusion when they realize the disorder and delay. All they wanted was to build their dream home. Why was it becoming more like a nightmare? What went wrong? The answers to these questions are relatively simple. There was no team, no organization, no coordinated effort, and no complete design process.

Figure 3.6

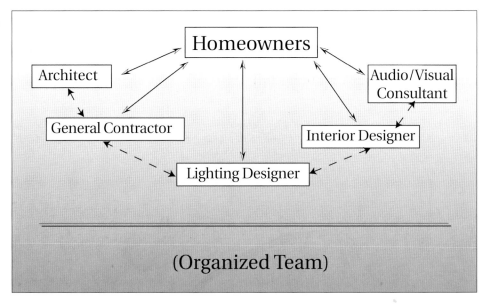

THE NEW PROCESS: THE TEAM APPROACH

The team approach should be utilized to avoid the conflicts presented by the above scenario. Communication and an organized execution of the building process can relieve much of the stress associated with home building. As with any team, each member has a specific role that is defined prior to the process. The design team consists of the following team members and their respective disciplines.

- The Homeowners
- The Architect
- The General Contractor
- The Interior Designer
- The Lighting Designer
- The Audio/Video Consultant
- The Security Consultant
- The Communications and Data Network Specialist
- The Electronic Architect
- The Kitchen and Closet Designer
- The Landscape Architect
- The Electrical Engineer, for homes above 8,000 square feet

The role of each team member is diverse and unique.

The Homeowners

The owners need to be as educated in the new design and building process as soon as possible (i.e., utilization of audio/video systems, lighting control systems, telephone systems, data and network communication systems). They should generate a wish list of the home's style, features, use and amenities. Color photographs, magazine pieces and design styles should be collected for visual reference. The owners should gather specifics regarding room functions (e.g., bedroom with specific illumination for reading; master shower with steam capability; kitchen with two dishwashers and commercial style range; media room with hidden projector screen; bathroom and kitchen floors with radiant heating; entire home to have high speed data and network distribution systems for telecommuting). Prior to beginning, it is important for the owners to set budget guidelines that do not sacrifice quality. The owners should be involved in the team's decision-making process. Nobody likes surprises, especially when they are paying the bills. Owners need to insist on a collaborative team process from the inception of the project.

The Architect

The architect is responsible for the building design, which includes interior and exterior design concepts, overall building heights, floor to floor heights, and site placement. The home's design should have adequate mechanical compartments for electrical panels, lighting panels, audio/video equipment, telephone distribution boards and chases for wiring, plumbing and mechanical ducts. General electrical items to be noted on the plans include outlet locations and appliance circuit layouts. The exterior building finishes and roofing materials, as well as window and door selection, should be specified on the documents. If requested, floor systems to accommodate radiant heating should be provided with the plans. Building material specifications (i.e., trusses, steel beams, framing details, exterior wall sheeting, and foundation treatments) should be itemized in the design package. The architect's work should be in compliance with local building department codes and regulations. All efforts and budgets are coordinated with the team leader (the general contractor) to ensure ease of construction practices. Site observation, team meeting attendance throughout the building process, and modifications as necessary to the architectural drawings are also the architect's responsibilities. The architect should recommend an experienced residential interior designer, lighting designer, and electronic architect for presentation to the homeowners and for team inclusion. He or she correlates the interior design, lighting concepts, and electronics into the architectural spaces.

Figure 3.7

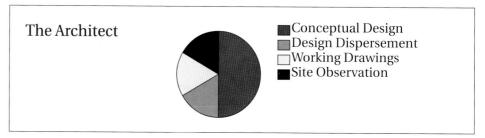

The General Contractor

The <u>leader</u> of the team, the general contractor, is responsible for the ultimate selection of the subcontractors (i.e., electrical contractor, plumbing/mechanical contractor, roofing contractor, etc.) and coordination of all design implementation by subcontractors. He or she schedules the subcontractors' and consultants' site reviews and determines the critical path scheduling for work tracking and completion. The general contractor reviews and approves all subcontractor billing prior to submission to the owners for payment and compiles all of the budgets. He or she also recommends specialists in the design and construction process to the homeowners and architect.

Figure 3.8

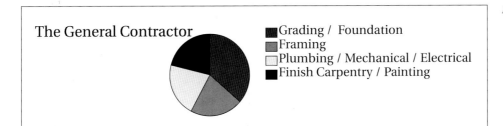

The General Contractor

- ▨ Grading / Foundation
- ▥ Framing
- ▢ Plumbing / Mechanical / Electrical
- ■ Finish Carpentry / Painting

The Interior Designer

The interior designer is responsible for seeing that the homeowners' design wishes are fulfilled to their satisfaction. This skill entails consideration in a variety of areas: design and finishes of reflected ceiling plans; furniture plans, including selection and placement; wall details; color palette of all rooms; fireplace, molding, door, and counter top designs; initial cabinet design, including function and finishes; tile layout and specification; selection of flooring materials; decorative lighting fixture selection and placement (coordinated with lighting designer); plumbing fixture selection; custom window application and treatments (i.e., drapery, drapery motors, black-out shades, blinds, pocket doors); artwork coordination with homeowners; and, correlation of materials, finishes and furniture budgets. The interior designer coordinates with the team leader in phase scheduling and communicates the need for any additional construction supports for artwork, stonework, and other elements. He or she coordinates with all team members to ensure success in the implementation of the team's specified products.

Figure 3.9

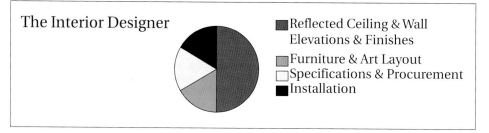

The Lighting Designer

The lighting designer is responsible for the communication and education of the homeowners in lighting products, effects, energy usage, maintenance and aesthetics. Other responsibilities include: complete design and engineering of the lighting control system; production of lighting design plans that incorporate floor plans; reflected ceiling plans; interior designer's furniture plans (if available); art placement; and, details showing the special integration of lighting equipment into the architecture, furnishings and cabinetry. Detailed fixture specifications should also be included in these plans. Correlation with other team members and meeting attendance are critical, as well as site observation and final lighting and control adjustments. Assistance in preparing budgets for the lighting and control package is also important, as is client training on the lighting control system at project completion. The lighting designer should not supply any lighting or control products to avoid conflict of interest in the product specifications. The lighting designer's ultimate goals should be to design attractive lighting effects for the interior and exterior of the project and to work cohesively with the other team members.

Figure 3.10

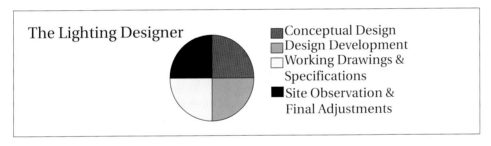

The Audio/Video Consultant

It is the audio/video consultant's responsibility to educate clients regarding what products will fulfill their requests and budget requirements. The A/V consultant should consider the products' upgrade capabilities for new technology, and all pre-writing should accommodate these fast moving changes. The consultant should not be product-driven but client-driven in motivation. He or she coordinates all speaker and equipment locations with the team members to avoid spatial conflicts. The A/V consultant must spend substantial time with the cabinet maker, electrical contractor, and lighting designer to ensure product coordination with equipment racks, built-in video walls, and other entertainment areas. The A/V consultant should attend all team meetings and follow the team leader's instructions and time lines. Site observation, construction adjustments, and final client training in equipment operations are essential. It is important that the consultant be willing and able to work in tandem with the lighting designer, electronic architect, electrical and other contractors involved with low-voltage wiring. Convergence requirements involving audio/video, Internet access, PC/TV, telephone, data, and fax sub-systems must be coordinated between team members.

Figure 3.11

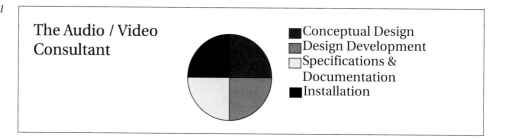

The Audio / Video Consultant

- Conceptual Design
- Design Development
- Specifications & Documentation
- Installation

The Security Consultant

The security consultant's services fulfill the safety requirements of the client. Typical items reviewed during the security design process are: security lighting, either on motion detectors or sensors (coordinated with the lighting consultant); panic buttons throughout the home to trigger lighting and audible alarms; glass breakage sensors; and, door openings monitored after the home is placed in a goodnight mode. Many of these items are coordinated with the electronic architect.

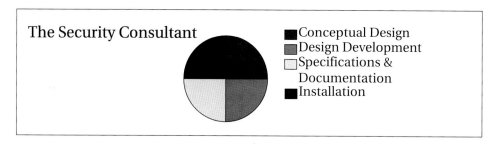

Figure 3.12

The Communications and Data Network Specialist

In today's fast-paced world of computer technology, a communications and data network specialist is important, if not critical, to the home's initial infrastructure wiring. The technology is currently available to incorporate the proper wiring into a residential environment. Examples include: providing high-speed data cabling for Internet access in every room; network wiring to link the home's personal computers; wiring to allow a television screen to act as a PC monitor; fiber optic cabling for rapid transferring of data; and, wiring for telecommuting which links the home to the office environment for video conferencing. It is important to realize that this specialist is in addition to the audio/video consultant and electronic architect.

Figure 3.13

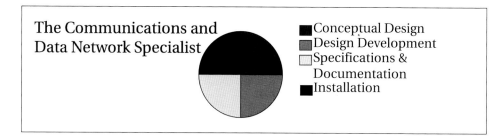

The Electronic Architect

The electronic architect, also known as the systems integrator, is responsible for the low-voltage system design and programming necessary for integration of all the intelligent electrical components distributed throughout the residence. Every electrical device that is installed in the home has a type of computer intelligence and the integrator connects these various devices (i.e., lighting control system, audio/video system, irrigation system, heating and air-conditioning system, fire and security systems, motorized devices, and computer networks). Through program language and additional specialty infrastructure wiring, these multiple devices can interface and talk to each other. These devices respond to controls such as key pads, wall mounted touch screens, hand held remote controls, motion triggered and timed products. The electronic architect adds a level of sophistication and simplicity in the everyday running of the electronic home by programming commands to all the electronics into one control panel. This approach has the benefits of cost savings, elimination of wall clutter, and simplification of use. This is perhaps the fastest growing design specialty in the residential building process today.

Figure 3.14

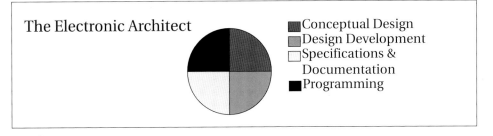

The Kitchen / Closet Designer

As mentioned above, the interior designer creates the outward appearance of the cabinetry. It is the kitchen / closet designer's responsibility to present all contemporary options to the homeowners, as well as provide the working drawings for construction. The kitchen/closet consultant should attend the team meetings as requested by the team leader. He or she should oversee the construction and installation of the cabinetry, as well as coordinate all special lighting considerations with the lighting designer.

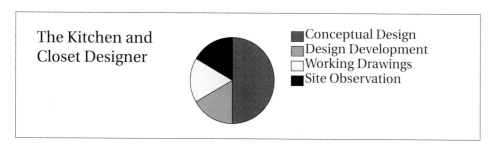

Figure 3.15

The Kitchen and Closet Designer

- Conceptual Design
- Design Development
- Working Drawings
- Site Observation

The Landscape Architect

It is the responsibility of the landscape architect to provide the design for everything that falls outside of the building architect's scope of work. Those areas include the hard scape: driveways; steps; patios; gazebos; swimming pool design and location; pool decks; pathways; stepping stones; planters; fountains; reflecting ponds; arbors; and, sculptural placement. These areas of focus are in addition to the plantings, trees, irrigation and soil selection for the site. The landscape architect also develops budgets that are included in the project's overall allowance. The landscape architect also works with the team to coordinate the lighting, irrigation and elements requested by the building architect, interior designer and lighting designer. The team objective in this area is to blend landscape with the overall design concept of the property and the dwellings.

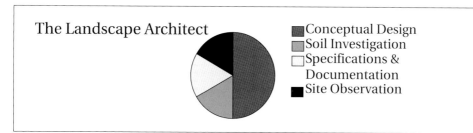

Figure 3.16

The Landscape Architect

- Conceptual Design
- Soil Investigation
- Specifications & Documentation
- Site Observation

The Electrical Engineer

The electrical engineer is responsible for locating and sizing the electrical service. Sizing is determined by the total connected load, lighting panel circuiting and distribution, and additional power related sub-panels. Responsibilities also include: calculations for convenience outlets; appliance circuiting based on specific appliance requirements (usually supplied by the kitchen consultant); and motors for skylights, window coverings, sump pumps, swimming-pool equipment, exterior lighting sub-panels; audio/video electrical requirements; elevators; back-up generators; surge suppression systems; and, network system requirements.

Figure 3.17

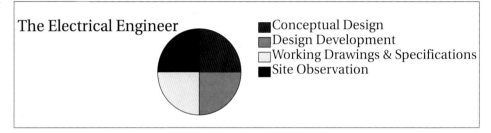

The Electrical Engineer

■ Conceptual Design
■ Design Development
□ Working Drawings & Specifications
■ Site Observation

Unfortunately, it has been unusual for electrical engineers to be included in the design of residences under 8,000 square feet. The reason for this omission is that the electrical contractor is unfairly expected to design, select and compile information that impacts his or her work. The electrical contractor does not customarily receive additional fees for this extra analysis and service.

The Electronic Drawing Coordinator

Another possible member that could be added to the team effort is the electronic drawing coordinator. He or she would gather the initial architectural, interior design, reflected ceiling, and furniture plans. He or she would then compile and immediately distribute the completed plans to each team member in order for the individual discipline to begin their design process. This additional member would also be responsible to keep all team members updated with changes as they occur throughout the design and building process.

Application of the team system from the beginning of the project is well overdue in the residential building process. Many projects may not begin with an established team, but the general contractor frequently takes the lead by default and gradually assembles the individual consultants. No matter what the cost or size of a residence, an organized general contractor and committed team players can create an outstanding home. A winning team concept prevents the homeowners' bewilderment over belated consultant fees and cost overruns. Every team player has his or her role defined within the project. One person is no longer responsible for all the design elements that create contemporary residences. The team approach clearly produces higher initial consultant costs when it is established at the beginning of the design process. Yet, the increased budget will practically eliminate additional service costs, change orders, upgrades and other unforeseen expenses.

The main reason this process will become industry standard is that owners are becoming more educated regarding the building process. They realize that one person or design discipline cannot begin to effectively design sophisticated systems, especially modern home electronics. In the past, home electrical and lighting needs were minimal and consisted of in-wall rotary dimmers, track lighting, and recessed eyeball-type fixtures. Audio/video systems consisted of a color television with a VCR and a stand alone stereo system. Home design and building processes need to comply with today's high-tech standards.

Technological advances are evident and ongoing in almost every industry. For example, when a consumer is in the market to purchase a new automobile, he or she expects certain items to be included in the package. The buyer wants features even though he or she may not completely understand the technology of: load leveling devices that balance heavy loads; a remote door access device that allows for locking and unlocking without fumbling for a key; a car alarm system; AM/FM and CD system with Dolby® and surround sound; automatic lighting systems to fade off and on upon exiting or activating the remote unlocking device; automatic seats and windows; and, multi-speed windshield wipers. On-board computer processors are the brains of the electrical and mechanical systems that monitor the auto fuel injection system, control the idle, deliver signals to the anti-lock brakes, and control the dashboard instrumentation. These additions increase the overall cost of the car, but they also add value and efficiency.

It has been said that the two most important and expensive purchases that are made in a lifetime are the home and the automobile. Contemporary design of the residential environment should be rivaling advancements in auto technology. However, the features offered in the majority of today's new homes are the same as those offered in homes 20 to 30 years ago. Proven technology and services are available for the mass market, so why not expect something more?

Part 2

The Process and Practice of Residential Lighting Design

CHAPTER FOUR

Organizing the Design Documents

Professional drawings and documents are critical because they illustrate the designer's intention on the job site and dictate the design's execution. The overall success of the project is jeopardized when a plan is hastily completed or lacks sufficient information. The practice of lighting design had a precarious beginning because talented, visually oriented lighting designers did not take the time or spend the funds to prepare professional lighting plans and documents. Lighting design does not consist of peel-off colored dots on the architectural plans, rough sketches, or arm waving on the job site. These types of practices diminish the professionalism of the team.

The following process organizes the team documents into an easily understood lighting design package. This organizational method was greatly improved with the introduction of computer drawing programs which have revolutionized drafting in the architectural and engineering community.

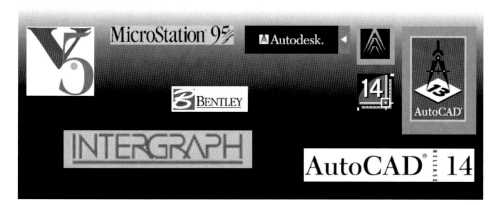

*Figure 4.1
Common computer drafting
tools.*

Prior to these programs' introduction, all drawings were hand drafted (a very tedious and time consuming process). As with most technological advances, it is a wonder that architectural and lighting design plans were ever produced without this great tool.

The use of computers was initially slow to be adopted by the industry. However, many members of contemporary design teams coordinate entire sets of documents by sending disks via express mail services or by electronically transferring information via modem. This exciting utilization of computers and technology allows the team members to be dispersed around the country and world without missing a beat.

Figure 4.2
Linking computers throughout
the United States has proven to
be a successful design team tool .

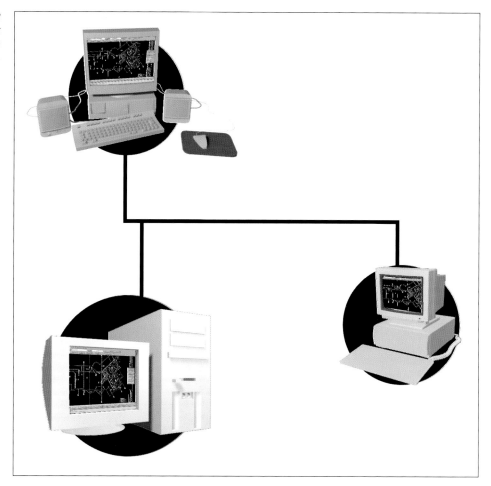

The following is a check list of items required by the lighting designer to begin assembly of the lighting documents.

From the architect:

Floor plans

Reflected ceiling plans (if not provided by the interior design)

Interior building sections

Exterior elevations

Structural plans

Specialty lighting requests

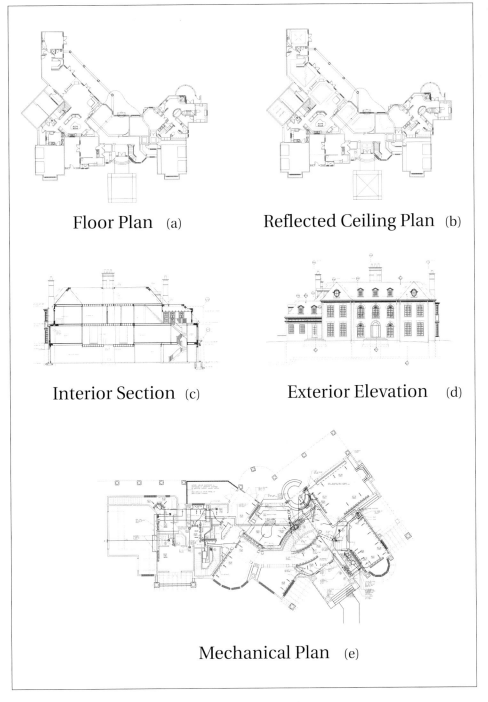

Floor Plan (a)

Reflected Ceiling Plan (b)

Interior Section (c)

Exterior Elevation (d)

Mechanical Plan (e)

Figure 4.3
(a) Floor plan.
(b)Reflected ceiling plan.
(c)Interior section.
(d)Exterior elevation.
(e)Mechanical plan.

From the interior designer:
    Furniture layout
    Reflected ceiling plans (if in their scope)
    Interior wall elevations (if in their scope)
    Art work placement
    Cabinet drawings and details
    Wall colors and floor finishes
    Specialty lighting requests

Figure 4.4
Furniture and artwork place-
ment plan.

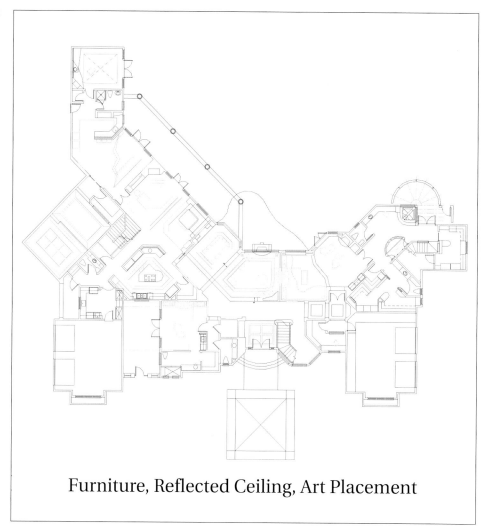

Furniture, Reflected Ceiling, Art Placement

From the audio/video consultant:
  Wall and ceiling speaker locations
  Equipment rack locations
  Video projectors locations
  Control device locations in walls and furniture

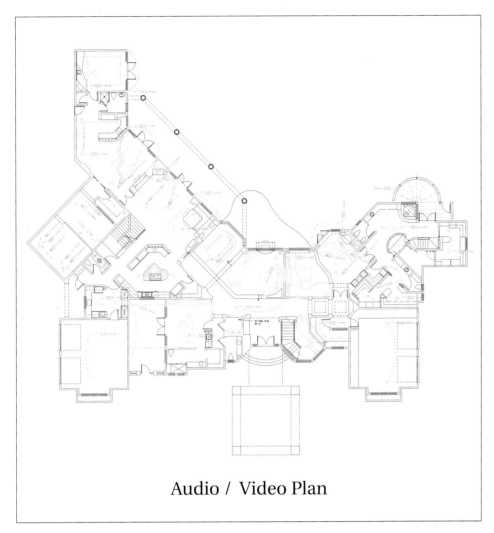

Figure 4.5
Audio/Video plan.

Audio / Video Plan

From the security consultant:
    Motion sensor locations
    Exterior eve lighting locations
    Security monitor locations
    Camera locations
    Powered shelf and racks locations

*Figure 4.6
Security plan.*

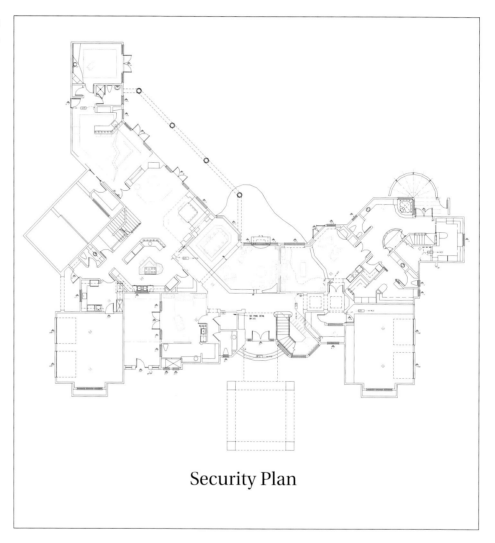

Security Plan

From the communication and data network specialist:
Equipment rack locations
Wall device locations
Interface equipment requirements

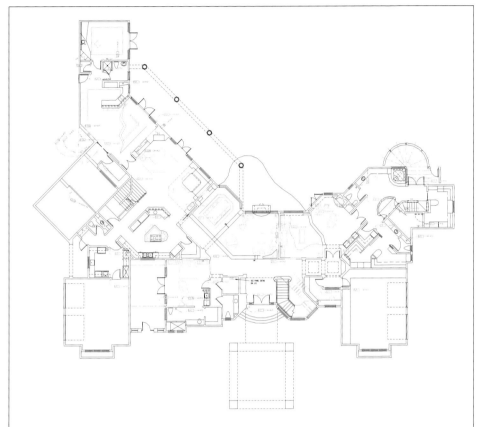

Communication and Data Network Plan (a)

Figure 4.7
Communication and data
network plan.
(a) Control plan
(b)Rack / Outlet detail

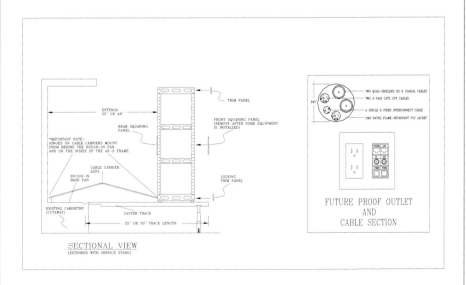

Rack / Outlet Detail (b)

From the electronic architect:
  Interface equipment selection
  Equipment rack locations
  Motion sensor locations

Figure 4.8
Electronic
architect plan.

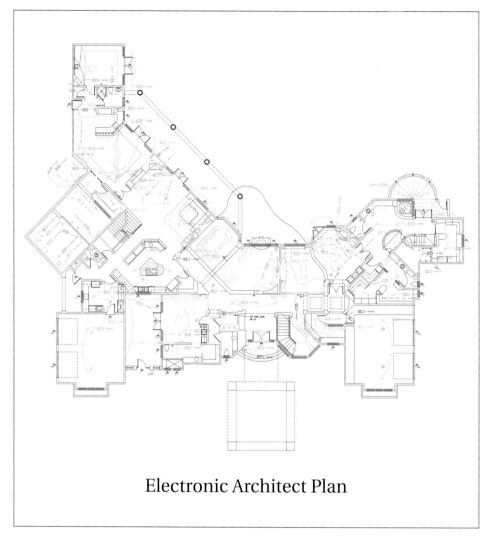

Electronic Architect Plan

From the kitchen and closet designer:
    Floor plan drawings locating cabinetry
    Elevated drawings
    Specialty lighting requests

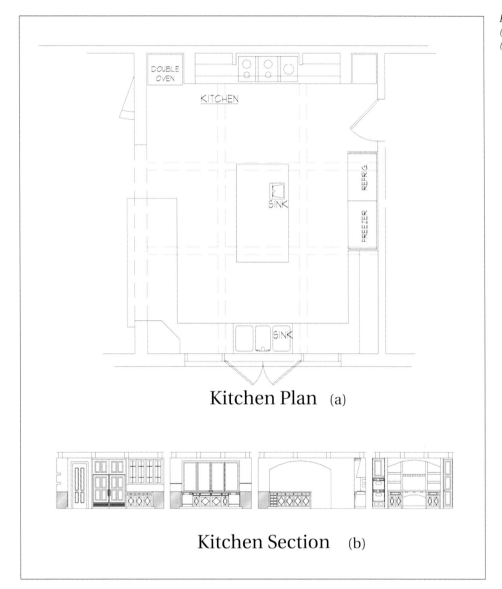

Figure 4.9
(a) Kitchen cabinet layout.
(b)Kitchen cabinet elevation.

As the team approach becomes prevalent in the home design and building industry, this information will then be available prior to beginning the lighting design process. A lighting designer must at least have the architectural and interior design documents to begin the drawing organization.

DRAWING ORGANIZATION STEPS

Once the above information has been gathered, the lighting designer must compile it into one document. A major strength of computer drawing programs is the layering technique, where several individual drawings are laid on top of one another. Prior to these computer programs, the floor and furniture plans were separate from the reflected ceiling plan. Now, this information can be merged into one plan which minimizes errors. The general and electrical contractors no longer need to reference several documents. Utilizing this process, one plan can be produced which contains individual elements on which to base the lighting plan:

Figure 4.10

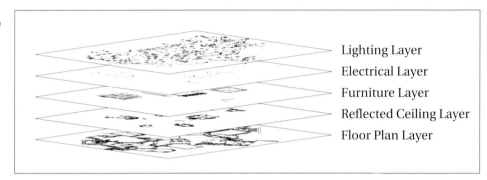

Lighting Layer
Electrical Layer
Furniture Layer
Reflected Ceiling Layer
Floor Plan Layer

The floor plan *layer* includes:
    Architectural floor plans
    Cabinet and counter layout
    Door locations and swing direction
    Window locations

Figure 4.11

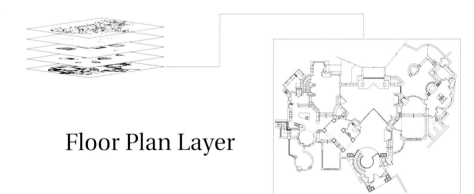

Floor Plan Layer

The reflected ceiling plan *layer* includes:
    Reflected ceiling design
    Ceiling height notations for each room
    Speaker locations
    Sprinkler head locations
    Smoke detector locations
    Mechanical vents and grills
    Eave outlines
    Dormer outlines

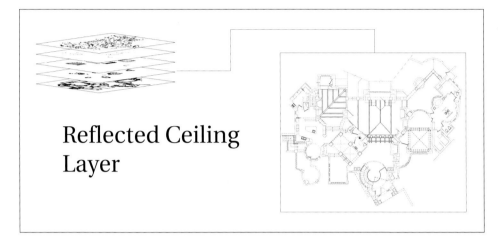

Figure 4.12

Reflected Ceiling Layer

The furniture plan *layer* includes:
    Sofa and chair locations
    Table locations
    Art locations
    Bedroom furniture location
    Floor and table lamp locations
    Carpet and area rug locations
    Armoire, hutch and buffet locations
    Specialty cabinet and furniture locations
    Floor materials information

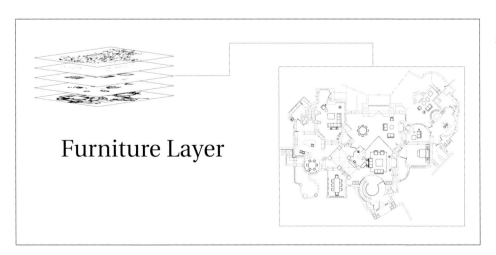

Figure 4.13

Furniture Layer

The electrical plan *layer* includes:

 Lighting control loops or switch legs
 Lighting control panels
 Lighting control keypads
 Low-voltage transformers
 Power panels
 Baseboard outlets switched on lighting control
 Floor outlets
 Top of mantel outlets

Figure 4.14

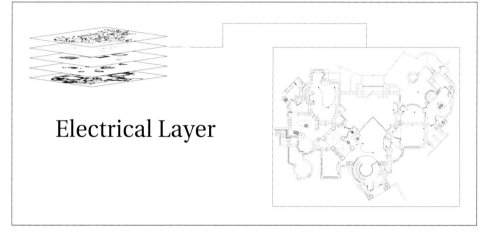

The lighting plan *layer* includes:

 Recessed lighting fixtures, including dimensions
 Ceiling decorative fixtures
 Wall sconce locations and heights
 Indirect cove lighting fixtures
 In-ground lighting fixtures
 Specialty wall up-lighting fixtures
 Fireplace hearth lighting fixtures
 Under cabinet lighting fixtures
 Interior cabinet lighting fixtures
 Top of cabinet lighting fixtures
 Specialty outlets for paintings

Figure 4.15

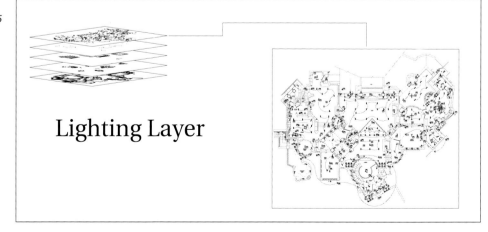

Each layer retains specialized information. They can be merged together and plotted or sent via modem to all of the team members. It is exciting to be able to turn off layers and plot only selected information. An example of this application would be to turn off the electrical layer, and only display the floor plan, furniture, reflected ceiling, and lighting layers, so the audio/video consultant can locate the ceiling speakers. More layers can be added if project information needs to be separated in greater detail — the possibilities are numerous. For example, the switch legs (control loops connecting the lighting to be switched) could merit a circuiting layer.

PLAN NOTES, SPECIFICATIONS, SYMBOLS AND DESIGNATIONS

Critical to the plan organization is the use of detailed plan notes, specifications and fixture symbols and designations. All of this information should be included in the drawing package and not in separate documents that could be detached from the plans and cause potential confusion for the installing contractor.

Plan notes refer to details with specific installation information, such as the incorporation of lighting into the architecture, cabinetry or furnishings.

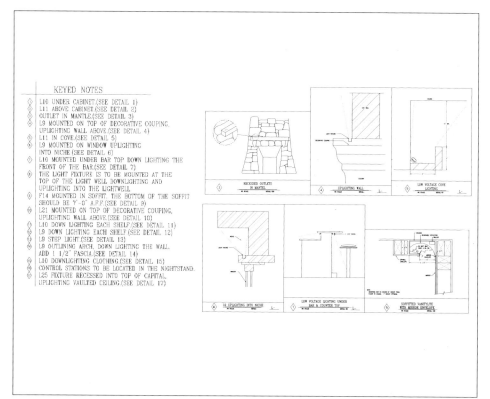

Figure 4.16
Plan notes and details.

Specifications consist of manufacturer catalogue numbers and lamp type information. Voltage, wattage, mounting and special lensing techniques are noted for all of the project's fixtures.

Figure 4.17
Lighting fixture schedule.

FIXTURE SCHEDULE

TYPE	MANUFACTURER	CATALOGUE NO.	MOUNT	VOLTS	WATTS	LAMP	LENS	LOUVRE
L1	HALO	H99ICT/993W	REC	120	50	GE PAR20/FL		
L2	HALO	H9ICAT/5001P	REC	120	60	GE PAR30/HIR/FL		
L3	HALO	H77/410W	REC	120	90	GE PAR38/HIR/FL		
L4	DREAMSCAPE	DLX-7005IC/7300D	REC	120/12	50	GE MR16/EXN	DL-7226	DL-7225
L4A	DREAMSCAPE	DLX 7005C/7300D	REC	120/12	35	GE MR16/ESX		
L5	LIGHTOLIER	B7054CL/8600	REC	120	150	A21		
L6	CSL	7002/DXIC	REC	120/12	50	GE MR16/EXT	-02	
L7	DREAMSCAPE	DLX-7005C/7300A	REC	120/12	50	G.E. MR16/EXT	DL-7226	
L8	ARTISTIC LIGHTING	OPTICAL FRAMING PROJECTOR	REC	120	250	QCLMC		
L9	ROBERTS STEP LIGHT	A SERIES-EB 2" O.C.	SURF	24	10W PER FT.			
L10	STARFIRE	XENFLEX 2" O.C. 5 WATT	SURF	24	30W PER FT	ZENON WEDGE	XF-L	
L11	STARFIRE	XENFLEX 3" O.C. 10 WATT	SURF	24	40W PER FT	ZENON WEDGE		
L12	DECORATIVE WALL SCONCE	BY OWNER/ INTERIOR DESIGNER	WALL	T.B.D	T.B.D	T.B.D		
L13	DECORATIVE CEILING FIXTURE	BY OWNER/ INTERIOR DESIGNER	PEND/SURF	T.B.D	T.B.D	T.B.D		
L14	LIGHOLIER	8172WH/6001WH/7515	REC	120	50	MR16		
L15	HALO	H4-T/40 ALBALITE	REC	120	70	A19		
L16	HALO	H2-T/25 ALL GLASS	SEMI REC	120	150	A21		
L17	RSA	C-50/MLV 3035	REC	120/12	50	G4		
L18	DREAMSCAPE	MOONSHADOW DLX 101/201/502/A	REC	12	35	MR16		
L19	DREAMSCAPE	MICROWELL DL130	GROUND	12	20	MR11		
L20	DREAMSCAPE	MESA DL	SURF	12	35	MR11	DIFFUSION	HONEYCOMB
L21	HYDREL	4842-3	GROUND	12	75	MR16		
L22	LUMENYTE	PH1000/WN500	SURF	120	250	QUARTZ HALOGEN		
L23	CSL	9881/5C	REC	12	35	G.E.MR16/ESX	-02	0-14
L24	HADCO	BC3-A/53A	SURF	120	100	G.E.PAR30/FL	CLEAR-INCLUDED	
L25	JUNO	TL2/TL103WH 6"O.C.	SURF	12	20	12V T3		
F1	LIGHTOLIER	13T42UU/13550AZ	SURF	120	80	SPX 30 SERIES		
F2	LIGHTOLIER	13244UU/13558AZ	SURF	120	80	SPX 30 SERIES		
F3	ALKCO	LITTLEINCH 213-S SF	SURF	120	26	2-T5		
F4	LIGHTOLIER	13222UU/13554AZ	SURF	120	80	2-U		
F14	CELESTIAL	VANITYLITE VAN10	REC	120	55W PER FT	BIAX 3500K		

Fixture symbols depict the type of lighting fixtures on a plan, whether mounted on the ceiling or wall, or recessed in the ceiling or floor. These symbols should also be tagged with a specific designation that refers back to the fixture specifications.

Figure 4.18
Lighting manufacturer
cut sheets.
(Photographer:
Andrew M. Mitchell, FPI)

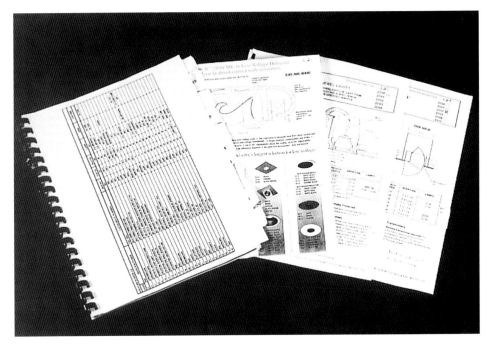

The lighting fixture specification binder includes manufacturers' cut-sheets, pictures or drawings showing dimensions, configurations, mounting requirements, and photometrics. This information is crucial to the installer during the procurement and framing process.

Regardless of the lighting designer's talent, his or her documents need to be precise and representative of a design professional. The documents should be easily understood by the client and the electrical contractor.

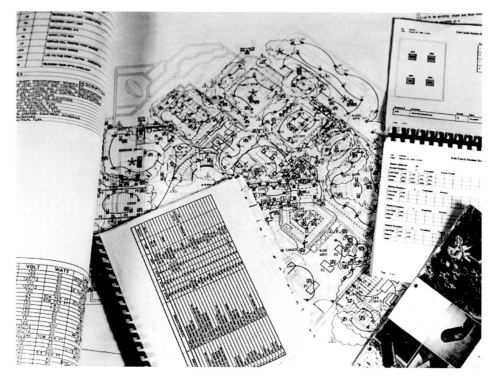

Figure 4.19
Precise lighting documents can prevent any miscommunication.
(Photographer:
Andrew M. Mitchell, FPI)

CHAPTER FIVE

The A.D.A.P.T.I.V.E. Method™

Once the background plans are compiled, the lighting designer can begin a detailed study of the other team members' information. Reviewing this material and beginning the lighting layout can be an overwhelming task, especially if the home is quite large. Deciding where to begin and which design aspects to concentrate on can make the process rather daunting. To make this process easier, I have developed an organized method that walks the designer step by step through the lighting layout. It is called The A.D.A.P.T.I.V.E. Method™.

The adaptive method is perhaps the most important element in the lighting design process. After years of practicing lighting design, I have developed a precise *trade marked* process of teaching this sometimes mysterious practice.

A	=	Architecture
D	=	Decorative
A	=	Art
P	=	Path
T	=	Task
I	=	Interior Decoration
V	=	View
E	=	Exterior

By following this method in approaching the lighting design of a residence or commercial space nothing will be lost or left out. Visualization, lighting products, architectural practice, construction methods and experience are the only absent ingredients left to this successful recipe.

The A.D.A.P.T.I.V.E. Method™

 rchitecture

First and foremost is an evaluation of the architectural plans, details, sections and style to determine what is appropriate to highlight, accent, and beautify the architecture. The architect has put his or her all into creating a wonderful environment for the homeowners. With this in mind, it is the lighting designer's responsibility to compliment the architecture, not distract from it. Lighting equipment should be carefully located so as to never detract from the artistic qualities of the home. This can be accomplished by hiding lighting fixtures within the architecture and by keeping their quantity and size to a minimum. The lighting designer should always verify architectural lighting concepts with the architect after careful review of the plans. Be sure the recommendations meet architectural standards prior to presenting them.

Figure 5.1
An example of illuminating
architectural elements.
(Karen and Richard
Gomez Residence)
(Photographer:
Andrew M. Mitchell, FPI)

Areas to Illuminate
Decorative ceilings
Coves
Columns
Niches
Exterior building facades
Skylights
Clerestory fenestration
Any other notable building feature

Recommended Lighting Products (see Chapter Seven)
Recessed, adjustable low-voltage accent lights
Linear strip lights
Recessed floor or ground well lights

Decorative

Decorative elements, such as wall sconces, chandeliers, and surface mounted ceiling fixtures, compliment the architecture through proper placement and selection. These decorative fixtures are the jewelry of the structure. It is imperative to remember that these ornamental items are just props and they are not intended to provide room or area illumination. The lighting designer needs to verify all decorative locations with the architect and the interior designer. Fixtures must be selected to compliment the interior design and furnishings of the home.

Figure 5.2
An example of decorative lighting placement. (Photographer: Andrew M. Mitchell, FPI)

Areas to Illuminate
Wall sconces flanking mirrors or other wall hangings
Wall sconces on either side of entry or door ways
Wall sconces on columns
Wall sconces inside wide archways
Chandelier over dining room table
Chandelier in entry
Chandelier in living room
Surface mounted ceiling fixture in bedrooms

Recommended Lighting Products
Wall sconces
Chandeliers
Surface mounted ceiling fixtures

Art

Next, the lighting designer evaluates the art walls and specific display areas as requested by the homeowners and interior designer. The architectural evaluation clearly reveals where the focal walls, galleries, etc. will be located in the site.

*Figure 5.3
An example of artwork
illumination.
(Photographer: John White)*

Areas to Illuminate
Focal walls
Galleries
Display shelves
Sculpture locations
Niches

Recommended Lighting Products (see Chapter Seven)
Recessed, adjustable low-voltage accent lights
Optical framing projectors
Standard wall washing lights
Small low-voltage strip lighting attached to the painting frame
(where applicable).

ath

The path illumination phase of the design is critical, but often overlooked. A path of lighting needs to be created throughout the house in order for the homeowners to move comfortably from one room to another.

Figure 5.4
An example of
pathway illumination.
(Photographer: Mary E. Nichols)

Areas to Illuminate
    Hallways
    Transition spaces between rooms
    Stairwells
    Entry ways

Recommended Lighting Products (see Chapter Seven)
    Recessed, non-adjustable/sloped ceiling down lights

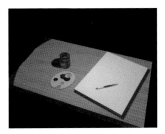

ask

Task illumination consists of incorporating lighting for specific work surfaces.

Figure 5.5
An example of task illumination.
(Photographer:
Andrew M. Mitchell, FPI)

Areas to Illuminate
>   Countertops
>   Cabinet interiors
>   Kitchen Islands
>   Baking Centers
>   Bathroom vanities
>   Laundry folding and ironing areas
>   Work benches
>   Specific reading and study areas
>   Stairs and landings
>   Bookcases

Recommended Lighting Products (see Chapter Seven)
>   Recessed, adjustable low voltage accent lights
>   Linear strip lights
>   Track lights, when recessed space is unavailable

Interior Decoration

Just like the architect, the interior designer utilizes his or her talents and abilities to develop an atmosphere that is compatible with the architecture and the homeowners' wishes. This phase of the lighting design process is as critical as illuminating the architecture.

Figure 5.6
An example of
interior decoration.
(Photographer:
Andrew M. Mitchell, FPI)

Areas to Illuminate

    Coffee tables & Dining tables

    Hutches & Armoires

    Carvings

    Murals

    Drapes

    Ornate tile or stonework

    Decorative mirrors

    Vases

    Interior plants

    Flower arrangements

    Other ornamentation

Recommended Lighting Products (see Chapter Seven)

    Recessed, adjustable low voltage accent lights

iew

Placement of the home on the lot is often dictated by a view. As the lighting designer adds adequate interior illumination by following the above steps, an undesirable image of the rooms' interiors are mirrored in every window. To soften this reflection, illumination should be added outside of the windows to draw the viewer's eye past the glass to add a visual extension to the room.

Figure 5.7
An example of
exterior illumination which
enhances the view.
(Carole and Jerry Turk
Las Vegas Residence)
(Photographer:
Chawla Photography)

Areas to Illuminate
Exterior of all notable windows

Recommended Lighting Products (see Chapter Seven)
Recessed, adjustable low- voltage accent lights

xterior

Exterior building and landscape illumination can be as exciting as the interior lighting process. Exterior lighting design (like architecture and interior illumination) can create a mood and atmosphere with a subtle, warm glow that welcomes the homeowners and visitors. It is important to consider many items and areas in the landscape lighting design process, such as the views discussed above, plus those listed below. The same principles of The A.D.A.P.T.I.V.E. Method™ apply to exteriors.

Figure 5.8
An example of
exterior illumination.
(Photographer: Arthur Coleman)

Areas to Illuminate
Distant focal points
Planting and color beds
Fountains
Pools
Reflecting ponds
Arbors
Gazebos
Paths
Sculpture

Recommended Lighting Products (see Chapter Seven)
Surface mounted lights

Once the lighting designer understands and is ready to apply The A.D.A.P.T.I.V.E .Method ™, the lighting plans can be created and implemented for the project.

ADAPTIVE METHODS™ IN MOTION

Figure 5.9
This Rocky Mountain home is
an excellent example of the
incorporation of the
ADAPTIVE Method™.
A. cove and niche lighting,
D. chandelier, wall sconces and
lamps, A. painting illumination,
P. path way illumination, T. cab-
inet work surface and interior
book case illumination, I. coffee
table and drapery accent light-
ing, V. exterior eave lighting,
E. exterior lighting in planting
area outside window.
(Photographer:
Andrew M. Mitchell, FPI)

Figure 5.10
This rustic log home again has
all the ADAPTIVE Method™ ele-
ments. A. indirect illumination
from concealed sources routed in
the log beam, D. chandeliers,
wall sconces and lamps,
A. art and artifact illumination,
P. area lighting for movement
through the room, T. bar top and
cabinet top illumination,
I. coffee table and end
table illumination,
V. eave lighting to draw eye
beyond the windows, E. exterior
illumination beyond.
Photographer:
Andrew M. Mitchell, FPI)

Figure 5.11
This elegant gallery is another
excellent example of the value of
the ADAPTIVE Method™ even in
*a small space. **A.** ceiling illumi-*
*nation in crown moldings, **D.***
*none, **A.** sculpture illumination,*
***P.** dramatic pathway to focal art,*
***T.** top of furniture illumination,*
***I.** front of furniture illumination,*
V.** uplights on exterior arch, **E.
accent lights on exterior
planting.
(Photographer: Andrew M.
Mitchell, FPI)

CHAPTER SIX

Creation and Implementation of the Lighting Design

The lighting design process can be categorized into eight steps. These steps organize the creation and implementation of the lighting design plans into a functional program, help monitor the overall process, and aid in presenting the design to the owner and team members.

Step 1: Initial Client Presentation
Step 2: Preliminary Design Phase
Step 3: Design Development Phase
Step 4: Construction Observation and Inspection Phase
Step 5: Control Station Design Phase
Step 6: Lamping Schedule Phase
Step 7: Construction Adjustment Phase
Step 8: Final Adjustments Phase

STEP 1:   THE INITIAL CLIENT PRESENTATION

Initially, the lighting designer meets with the owners to gain insight into their lighting and control needs. The designer presents photographs of related architectural and interior lighting applications to the clients to help them visualize possibilities for their own home. This meeting allows the clients to become part of the design process and allows the designer to note any of their special requests.

Figure 6.1
Initial client presentation.
(Video clip by
Andrew M. Mitchell, FPI)

This meeting is also an opportune time to discuss lighting control needs. This discussion will help the owners solidify and prioritize their requirements. For example, security may be a top concern for one client, while another ranks system flexibility high on the list, and another requires complete simplicity. While many lighting controls can accommodate all of these requests, the owners' responses give the lighting designer clues to important expectations.

The lighting designer's next step is to begin the actual lighting layout based on the information from the clientele.

STEP 2: THE PRELIMINARY DESIGN PHASE

This phase is the culmination of The A.D.A.P.T.I.V.E. Method™ of lighting design coupled with the owners' specific needs and wishes. The following is an outline of the tasks to be performed during this phase.

Project Review and Research

- Visual tasks
- Space function
- Color quality
- Daylight analysis
- Glare control
- Maintenance characteristics
- Reflectance/texture
- Luminance ratios
- Visual comfort probability
- Visual composition

Generation of Computerized Architectural Plans

It should be required that the lighting designer regenerate the architectural plans on computer if electronically drafted plans (disk or E-mail) are not readily available from the architect (see Chapter Four: *Organizing the Design Documents*). This will support the clarity and consistency of the lighting plans throughout the project and help convert the team to this powerful communications medium.

Preliminary Lighting and Related Electrical Layout

The final step in the Preliminary Design Phase is the incorporation of the initial project review and research into the architectural backgrounds generated on the computer drafting program. The following items are included in this step:

- lighting plans with control loops
- preliminary lighting fixture specifications and cut sheets
- relevant interior elevations

- notes on lighting control system being considered
- lighting details as needed
- switch locations
- motion control locations
- wall and floor receptacles switched through the control system
- motors, such as exhaust fans, paddle fans, drapery and skylights on control system
- cost estimates and budgets

Additional items are included depending upon design complexity:

- point-by -point luminance calculations
- shadowing effects
- luminance ratios
- computerized virtual walkthroughs
- computerized still renderings
- three dimensional photometric analysis

Team Presentation 1

Once all of the above items have been compiled into the computer drafted documents, it is time to present the preliminary lighting design plan to the homeowners and the design team. This meeting usually lasts three to four hours depending on the size and complexity of the home. The architectural and interior design presentations commonly include sample flooring, stone types, fabrics, color boards, photographs and other visual aids to convey design intent to the owners. The lighting designer should do the same by presenting samples of the following: lighting fixtures; lamp types; and, lighting control stations or key pads. Clients understand and respond to these visual tools.

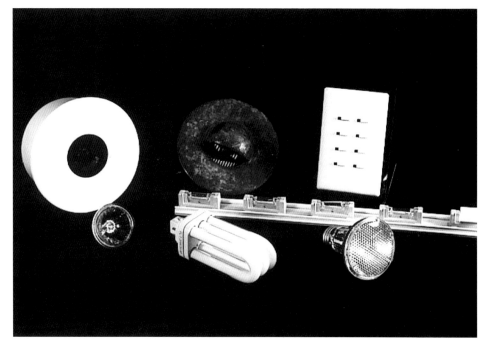

Figure 6.2
Product samples for the lighting presentation.
(Photographer: Andrew M. Mitchell, FPI)

They can actually feel the products and ask questions about colors, maintenance, and flexibility, rather than having to look at a cut sheet from a lighting catalog. Line drawings of specific lighting applications (with accompanying photographs of similar installations) will also keep confusion to a minimum.

Figure 6.3
Specific lighting
application detail.

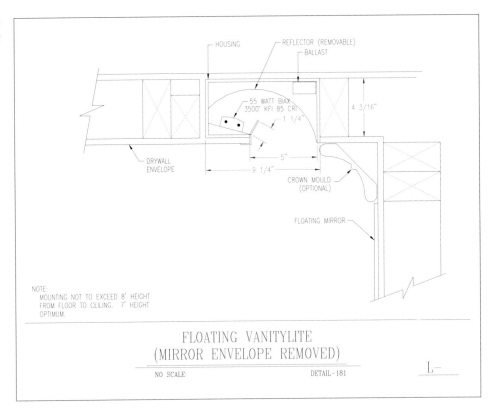

HOUSING
REFLECTOR (REMOVABLE)
BALLAST
55 WATT BIAX
3500° KFI 85 CRI
1 1/4"
4 3/16"
DRYWALL
ENVELOPE
5"
9 1/4"
CROWN MOULD
(OPTIONAL)
FLOATING MIRROR

NOTE:
MOUNTING NOT TO EXCEED 8' HEIGHT
FROM FLOOR TO CEILING.   7' HEIGHT
OPTIMUM.

FLOATING VANITYLITE
(MIRROR ENVELOPE REMOVED)

NO SCALE: DETAIL-181   L-

Visual aids strongly support presentation of the Preliminary Lighting Phase and clarify owner expectations.

Introduce the owners to their home in a systematic manner as it appears on the lighting plans; start at the front entry and move through the house.

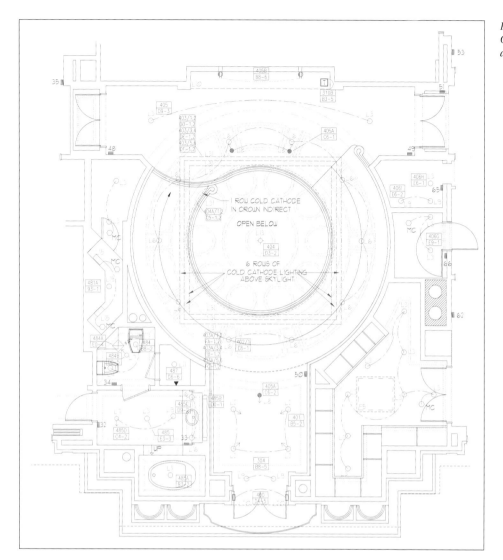

Figure 6.4
Combined architectural, interior and lighting plan.

This is a very interesting process for the clients to go through, as they imagine with assistance the lighting effects proposed by the designer. This is probably the first time the clients and the team are seeing a complete set of plans – consequently, it is difficult to keep the team focus solely on the lighting presentation. Questions arise about architecture and interior design as everyone reviews the plans. The documents designate location of the lighting and related electrical items, show the furniture layout, and note the reflected ceiling plan by the interior designer. The plans provide layered information and make it easy to explain the lighting effects as they relate to the furniture layout, the artwork placement, and the architecture. Likewise, it is easy to mark changes on the plans as the discussion continues between team members. Changes will take place, not only to the lighting portion of the plan, but also to the architecture and interior design as the process goes forward.

Next, the lighting designer should discuss the selected lighting control system and its varied uses, flexibility and cost effectiveness. The control system chosen should fulfill the clients' requests made at the initial presentation. The lighting and lighting control equipment budgets need to be presented and discussed at this point. The budget presentation is delayed only when changes are so extensive that products and quantities are significantly altered – thus, requiring a budget revision. As this presentation ends, the lighting designer will have sufficient direction to begin the Design Development Phase.

STEP 3:   THE DESIGN DEVELOPMENT PHASE

The Design Development Phase commences after the presentation and approval of the Preliminary Lighting Phase. The changes noted during the Preliminary Lighting Phase are made on the computer and a clean set of plans are plotted by the designer. The following is an outline of the tasks to be performed during the Design Development Phase.

Figure 6.5
The design development plan.

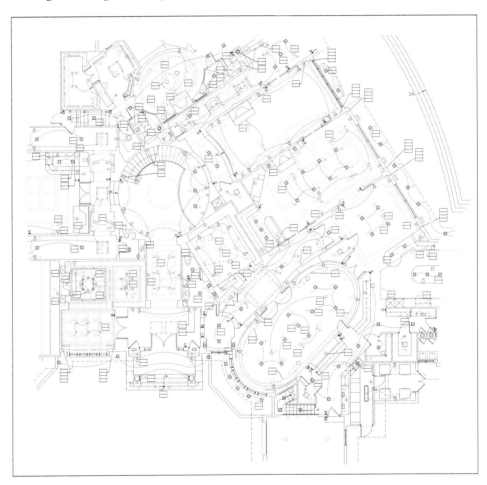

The Lighting and Control Plans

- Placement of lighting fixtures, completely dimensioned
- Placement of specialty lighting (i.e., artwork illumination)
- Placement of switched receptacles (outlets) related to the lighting
- Branch circuit wiring and control wiring, with load numbers
- Switch station or key pad locations, with identification numbers
- Lighting control enclosure locations and completed enclosure schedules
- Specialty lighting details for unique applications

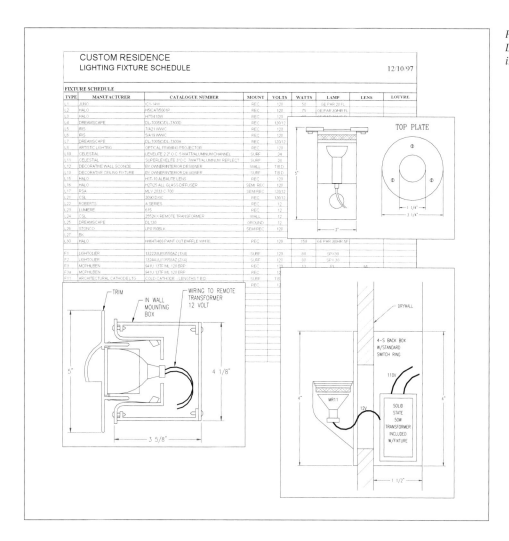

Figure 6.6
Lighting fixture specification
information.

The Specification Binder

This binder includes a lighting fixture schedule. The schedule contains the fixture designation, manufacturer, catalogue number, voltage, maximum wattage, specific lamp type and specialty lens or louver accessories for each specified product. Following the fixture schedule is a separate cut sheet with each product's specifications, such as physical size, voltage, mounting, use, etc. The lighting control enclosure data is also in this binder, along with an installation guide to direct the electrical contractor through his or her tasks.

Final Lighting and Control Budgets

Budgets based on the revised lighting and control plans can now be compiled for review. This information is obtained from the lighting and control manufacturer representatives assigned to the lighting designer's geographical area. The representative will supply contractor or list prices, depending on the designer's budgetary methods. Budget forms should show fixture quantities, price per unit and an extended price rather than a lump sum. It is important to note that the lighting designer should not be held responsible for these budget numbers (they are only estimates) in relation to the contractor's actual pricing.

Figure 6.7
Lighting fixture budget
worksheet.

"Client's Name"				
Estimated Costs				
Lighting and Fixtures & Control				
1/12/98				
Quantity	Type	Description	Price Per Fixture	Extended
1	L1	HALO H99ICAT/93GW	53.00	53.00
7	L2	HALO H5ICAT/5001P	33.00	231.00
18	L3	HALO H7T/410W	27.00	486.00
48	L4	DREAMSCAPE DL7005IC/7300D/7225	180.00	8,640.00
14	L5	DREAMSCAPE DL7005IC/7300D/7225	180.00	2,520.00
35	L7	DREAMSCAPE DL7005IC/7300A	170.00	5,950.00
12	L9	CSL DXIC/7002	216.00	2,592.00
48	L10	STARFIRE XENFLEX 2" O.C.	60.00	2,880.00
46	L11	STARFIRE XENFLEX 3" O.C.	63.00	2,898.00
9	L12	STARFIRE STARTUBE	9.65	86.85
18	L13	BY OWNER		
2	L14	D'LIGHTS 349-1/C-99	297.00	594.00
2	L15	BY OWNER		
1	L16	HALO H4T/40 ALBALITE LENS	63.00	63.00
6	L17	HALO H2T/25 ALL GLASS DIFFUSER	97.00	582.00
2	L18	HALO H7T/70PS	33.00	66.00
2	L19	BY OWNER		
2	L20	DREAMSCAPE DL126	205.00	410.00
6	L21	CSL 2552	99.00	594.00
6	L22	CSL 9681/DXIC	100.00	600.00
1	F14	CELESTIAL VANITYLITE VAN10	1,300.00	1,300.00
				-
				-
				-
				-
				-
				-
				-
				-
				-
				-
				-
				-
				-
				-
				-
This is an estimated budget only;			Total $	30,545.85
It does not incude decorative fixtures, fans, transformers,			Control +	25,460.00
labor, wire or sales tax.				$ 56,005.85

Team Presentation 2

Figure 6.8
Presenting the lighting plans
to the team.
(Video clip by
Andrew M. Mitchell, FPI)

This is the final presentation of the lighting, control and related electrical items that pertain to the home prior to construction. The meeting usually lasts only a few hours because everyone essentially agrees with the product placement, selection, and budgets (pending changes) reflected in the Design Development drawings. Once everyone is reasonably comfortable with the lighting design, a full lighting package (plans, details and specification binder) is issued to all of the team members and the owners. The electrical contractor will base the pricing, layout and installation of the lighting fixtures on data from this package. This information also dictates how the electrical contractor will terminate the switch legs or lighting fixture circuits into the lighting control enclosures (detailed in the specification binder). At the close of the meeting, the final lighting and control budgets should be presented to the owners for their budgeting purposes. It is up to the owners to share these numbers with the rest of the design team. This data gives the owners a gauge against which they can judge the subcontractor's prices.

STEP 4:
THE CONSTRUCTION OBSERVATION AND INSPECTION PHASE

Once construction has started, it is imperative that the lighting designer inspect the project to ensure the correct implementation of the lighting plans. Time and effort is saved by walking the site with the installing contractor and a set of lighting plans. For example, during this walk through the lighting designer may notice a fixture or control station has been covered up by plaster. The designer's attention to detail eliminates costly efforts to locate these items at a later date. Prior to final closing is a perfect time to make any necessary changes or adjustments to the lighting (due to structural limitations or architectural changes). The following is a check list of items to be inspected at the time of rough-in wiring.

Figure 6.9
Construction review is impera-
tive to the project's success.
(Video clip by
Andrew M. Mitchell, FPI)

Figure 6.10
As built changes are noted on
site, then drafted accordingly.
(Video clip by
Andrew M. Mitchell, FPI)

Rough-in Check List

Figure 6.11
Rough-in lighting and electrical
inspection.
(Carm and Nancy
Santoro Residence)
(Photographer:
Andrew M. Mitchell, FPI)

- Verify all lighting fixture locations and check off on the lighting plan
- Verify the distance from the wall to the installed fixture for all art accent lights
- Verify all decorative ceiling and wall locations, including heights
- Verify fixture placement and surface reflectance of coves and counter tops for lamp imaging problems
- Verify control station locations and check wiring
- Verify enclosure locations and check wiring loops
- If using a centralized processing control system, verify location, wiring and power feeds
- If using a distributed processing control system, verify wiring and supply feeds, if applicable
- Advise the electrical contractor to run a continuity check on all low-voltage wiring
- Verify that all switch legs are identified per drawing load numbering

STEP 5:   THE CONTROL STATION DESIGN PHASE

The Control Station Design Guide

The stations or key pads require design when a control system is specified in the plans. Up to this point, the stations have been located and numbered only on the lighting plans. The control station design is illustrated by a guide that depicts the recommended layout and custom engraving for each button or faceplate. This guide also includes the actual programming information and recommended button function for each station.

Figure 6.12
Information contained in a control station design guide.

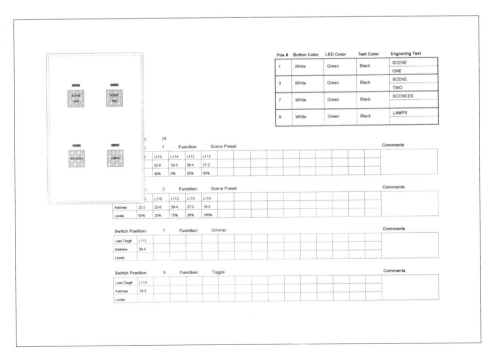

The following is an example of button function. Imagine the living room station's top left button (engraved "Scene One") controls the room's various circuits. The programming for this button might include the accent lighting at 70 percent intensity, the area lighting at 40 percent, the wall sconces at 25 percent, the indirect cove lighting at 50 percent and the floor lamps switched off. This is just one small example of the nuance that can be created with these systems. The items that should be addressed in the Control Station Design Guide are:

- Configuration of button layout
- Color and style of the device, usually dictated by the interior designer
- Engraving information
- Number of combined devices
- Load numbering, module and out-put labeling
- Pathway configuration
- Scene presets with percentages called out
- Owner's initial requests

The control station design guide should not be completed by the lighting designer until after the ceilings and walls are covered and the painting begins on the project. Stations are not designed and released for order with the rest of the lighting equipment during the Design Development Phase for several reasons. They probably would not be up to date due to subtle changes and would have to be returned at a restocking charge. Delaying the control design also saves time and money for the owner and the lighting designer. The changes to the architecture, interior design and, consequently, the lighting design have stopped by this phase.

Owner Presentation 3

The control station design guide should be presented to the owner at the time of painting and in the following manner. Each pictorial page of the design guide should be taped or otherwise attached over the wall opening of its corresponding control station. This method helps the owners visualize what each station controls and allows them to make desired revisions. Once the design has been approved, the owners should sign a release form, which allows the electrical contractor to order the stations. Once ordered, the keypads can be quickly produced and shipped.

STEP 6: THE LAMPING SCHEDULE PHASE

In the Preliminary Design and the Design Development Phases no specifications were noted regarding the characteristics of lamps used in lighting fixtures. The fixture schedule calls out only the lamp type and its maximum possible wattage (i.e., 50 watt MR16). Although the specifications can be closely predicted during the Design Development Phase, it is best to prepare the lamping schedule just prior to the painting process. The reasoning is twofold: 1) the lighting designer can actually feel and experience the space and volume for the first time in the walk through and evaluation; and, 2) the experienced lighting designer can accurately predict the lamps' effects and avoid numerous lamp changes during the Final Adjustment Phase. It is important that the electrical contractor be informed, early in the project, that the lighting designer will be producing a specific lamping schedule. The electrical contractor should include lamp costs in the bid based on preliminary information, knowing the lamps are firmly selected at a later date. He or she will need the lamping schedule soon after the home has been drywalled. This planning allows adequate time to prepare a material list and schedule for the trim-out phase of construction.

The lamping schedule consists of color coordinated mark-ups with a keyed legend that instructs the installers as to the exact wattage, beam spread, lens, diffuser or other special treatment needed for the specific task.

Figure 6.13
(a) An example of a lighting plan depicting a lamping schedule.
(b)Potential lamping accessories.
(Photographer:
Andrew M. Mitchell, FPI)

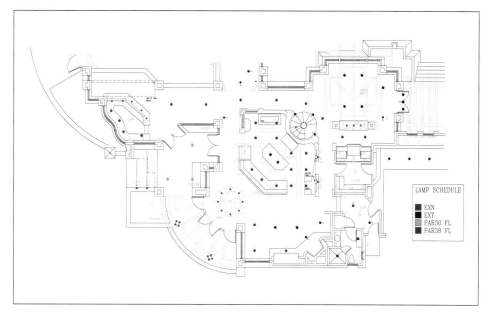

The cost and precise optical quality of the lamps and additional accessories are substantial budget items. The electrical contractor must ensure the protection of lamps from paint damage. If this type of damage occurs, the lamps will have to be replaced at an additional cost to the painting subcontractor.

STEP 7: THE CONSTRUCTION ADJUSTMENT PHASE

This is perhaps the most important phase of the project. Very little care is given to the adjustment of the fixtures once the electrical contractor installs the lamps according to the lamping schedule. The lighting designer is responsible for the focusing and adjustment of the lighting, not the electrical contractor.

Figure 6.14
Lighting construction adjustments with electrical contractor.
(Video clip by
Andrew M. Mitchell, FPI)

Some furniture and artwork may be in place by this time. Adequate attention to the project is required at this juncture, or else the lighting designer will be in trouble. At this point, the owners are becoming more excited about the home. They spend a great deal of time walking through with family and friends, and admiring the efforts of the team members. The walkthrough will be a disaster if early lighting adjustments are not complete. Instead of admiring the home, they will be distracted by uneven illumination, scallops of light on the walls, very dim or bright lamps, glare and numerous other problems. The owners will become upset and verbalize their concerns, as well as question the lighting design intentions. To avoid this scenario, the lighting designer must schedule a time to complete the construction adjustments prior to the owners' walkthrough appointment.

Not only are the lighting fixtures adjusted at this time, but the lighting control system is reviewed for proper function and settings. The lighting control representative should be called in to make any necessary adjustments if a control system malfunction is detected at this time.

*Figure 6.15
Hallway after construction
lighting adjustments (prior to
art placement).
(Photographer:
Andrew M. Mitchell, FPI)*

Construction Phase Check List

- Verify that all lamps are installed per the lamping schedule
- Verify that the lamps are free from paint, plaster and drywall compound
- Verify that all lighting fixture trims are located properly
- Verify that all specialty lenses or louvers are in place as specified
- Re-verify station locations and addresses
- Verify control station finish, engraving, button quality, display status
- Test override switching in enclosure modules
- Run a system diagnostics test to determine control station and load communication
- Verify programming is according to control station design guide

STEP 8:   THE FINAL LIGHTING ADJUSTMENTS PHASE

The real excitement takes place during the Final Lighting Adjustments Phase. This is when the clients can really see and feel the efforts of the meticulous lighting design process. Up to this point, they have been relying on the reputation and expertise of the lighting design professional. Now, for the first time, they can experience the long-awaited, professional results in their own home. Furniture and artwork should be permanently placed by this time.

It is advisable for the electrical contractor to physically direct the fixtures based on the lighting designer's instruction. This is largely due to insurance and liability concerns and the electrical contractor's familiarity with ladders, lifts and scaffolding.

(a)

(b)

In the Final Lighting Adjustment Phase, the following items are completed:

- Focusing the lighting on the intended objects
- Adding the necessary lens and louver combinations
- Re-lamping some areas for specific effects
- Adjusting the lighting levels for optimum effects

Figure 6.17
(a) Construction.
(b)Completion.
(Carm and Nancy
Santoro Residence)
(Photographer:
Andrew M. Mitchell, FPI)

(a)

(b)

Owner Presentation 4

The owners should be involved in the last few lighting adjustments. During this presentation, the re-lamping procedure and the adjustment of lighting fixtures can be demonstrated to them. This activity gives the owners the opportunity to understand the process and be able to re-lamp a fixture. This is also a good time for them to review and approve the final lighting effects that have been created by the designer. The lighting designer should walk through the entire home with the owners and explain each control station's button function and operation. The following is a control system check list for review.

Presentation of Control System Check List

- Demonstrate full dimming, toggle on/off, pre-set, fade up/down features
- Explain initial programming, re-programming and future programming capabilities
- Explain display options
- Explain telephone interface, if applicable
- Explain other available functions: vacation mode, away mode, welcome mode, asleep mode, timers, masters, combination locks
- Introduce the client to the lighting control manufacturer's representative
- Discuss who is responsible for the maintenance of the lighting control system
- Give the client a back-up disk and all related paperwork
- Present the client with a mini-set of laminated, as-built lighting and control plans
- Discuss that any additional programming changes will be billed at an hourly rate

The lighting designer is usually one of the last consultants to leave the project for the obvious reasons stated above. It is important that the homeowners feel comfortable with their home's lighting and control system. A follow up meeting three weeks to one month after the owners have moved in is strongly recommended to discuss any problems or concerns. This will add to the comfort level of all parties and ease any frustration that may exist in operating the system.

Part 3

The Products of Residential Lighting Design

CHAPTER SEVEN

Architectural Lighting Fixtures

Selection and placement of the lighting fixtures are perhaps the most important steps of the lighting design process. These elements are completely dependent upon the design criteria and structural limitations. Non-decorative lighting products can be broken into six categories and are distinguished by their ability to fulfill certain needs and provide specific effects.

The architectural lighting fixture categories include:

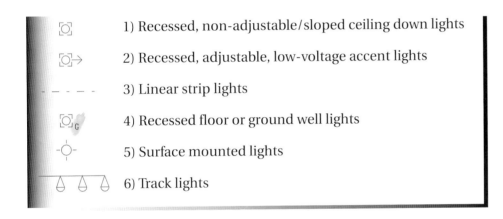

1) Recessed, non-adjustable/sloped ceiling down lights

2) Recessed, adjustable, low-voltage accent lights

3) Linear strip lights

4) Recessed floor or ground well lights

5) Surface mounted lights

6) Track lights

1) Recessed, non-adjustable/sloped ceiling downlights

Description: These fixtures, otherwise known as cans or high hats, are essentially recessed or flush mounted into the ceiling material. The common openings on the ceiling plane are approximately two, three, five, seven, and nine inches.

It is important that the placement of IC (insulated ceiling) and/or ICAT (air-tight) housings is verified with the local building and electrical codes.

Common usage: Recessed, non-adjustable fixtures are used to illuminate: kitchen work surfaces (islands, counter tops, sinks and interior cabinet lighting); desk areas; hallways; closets; garage work surfaces; and, bathroom vanities. The entry and porte-cochere, as well as the exterior perimeter of the house, can be lit with recessed down lights.

Figure 7.1
Recessed, non-adjustable lighting
trim samples.
(Photographer:
Andrew M. Mitchell, FPI)

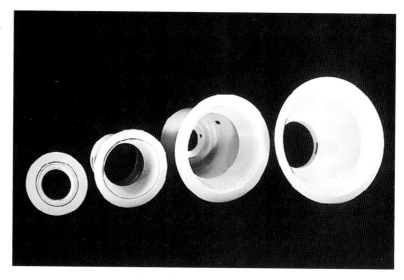

Voltages: 120, 120/12, 12 and 24

Placement: The placement varies depending on the specific task and selected lamp source (see Chapter 8). A good rule of thumb would be to view the spaces to be illuminated as area, path and task. The area and path lighting should be as even as possible without dark spots, unless required for intentional drama. The task lighting should be treated the same, but with brighter light levels. Most lighting manufacturer catalogs will give distribution information that is easy to understand.

Figure 7.2
Lighting manufacturer's lamp
distribution chart.

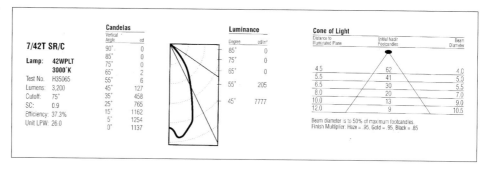

Graphics depict their product with a specific lamp type and its relative ceiling height. With this information, the lighting designer can overlay the lighting template specifications to ensure even coverage or utilize computer based programs that simulate the lamp and fixture performance as specified.

Figure 7.3
Graphic depiction of photometric
analysis.

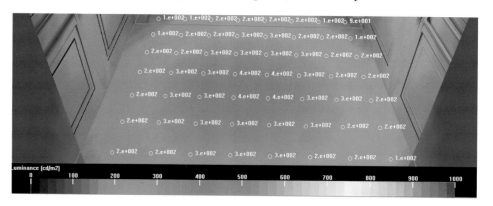

2) Recessed, adjustable, low-voltage accent lights

Description: The technology and terminology used with the recessed, adjustable, low-voltage accent light can be confusing. In the majority of residential applications there are two types of fixtures installed: integral and remote (referring to the transformer location). The most prevalent, the integral recessed, low-voltage fixture includes a step-down magnetic, electronic or torodial transformer.

*Figure 7.4
Recessed low-voltage housings.
(Photographer:
Andrew M. Mitchell, FPI)*

Transformers take the supplied 120 volt current and reduce it to 12 volts (the lamps are configured to operate at this voltage). What this means is that these fixtures install and wire the same as the recessed 120 volt down lights mentioned above. The only difference is the on-board, step-down, low-voltage transformer. The remote recessed, low-voltage fixture does not have an on-board transformer. Instead, the transformer is remoted in a nearby, accessible location. This product would be selected for installation in shallow or difficult areas with structural constraints, interior cabinet lighting and areas that are sound sensitive (due to the slight noise produced by some magnetic and electronic transformers). The use of torodial integral transformers in sound-sensitive areas has been very successful. The performance of both of these fixtures are due to the lamps for which they were designed: the ever flexible and energy efficient MR16 and MR11 low-voltage lamps. Low-voltage AR and PAR36 lamps can also be used in larger aperture recessed accent fixtures (see Chapter 8). It is important that the placement of IC (insulated ceiling) and/or ICAT (airtight) housings is verified with the local building and electrical codes.

Common usage: The recessed, adjustable, low-voltage accent light is utilized in the following ways: artwork illumination (paintings and sculptures) and interior furnishing illumination (coffee tables, clocks, flower arrangements, bookcases, armoires, end tables, dining room tables).

In the architectural arena, these fixtures are used to illuminate columns, doors, friezes, pass throughs, interior planters, steps, fountains, water features, built-in cabinetry and in eaves.

Figure 7.5
Samples of recessed
adjustable trims.
(Photographer:
Andrew M. Mitchell, FPI)

Voltages: 120/12, 12

Placement: As with recessed-down lights, the task at hand determines the use, lamp source and location of the product (see Chapter 8). Placement of fixtures, particularly art accents, is often troublesome for non-professional lighting designers. This is due to their lack of experience and interest in learning how to read the manufacturers' design specifications (which can be very confusing). The design specifications are established by an engineering department and based on complex equations that determine distance based upon ceiling height and fixture adjustability.

Figure 7.6
Imaginary string-line method for
determining fixture location.

Angle

In response to these factors, some simple rules of thumb can be helpful to the professional. If at all possible, determine the height, width and finish of the painting or sculpture to be illuminated. If this information is not available, the lighting designer can get very close by evaluating the space on plan or, better yet, on site. Pull an imaginary string line from the center of the adjustable low-voltage light fixture to the center of the object being lit.

Measure the degree angle and make sure that the fixture has the adjustability and full lamp image that is required according to the specifications. (See chart based upon 45 degree adjustability and full lamp image; also refer to Chapter 15 on art illumination).

3) Linear strip lights

Description: Linear strip lights are simply as the name states. These products have small individual lamps (see Chapter 8) at various spacing along a flexible molded extrusion with an internal ribbon or standard copper conductors.

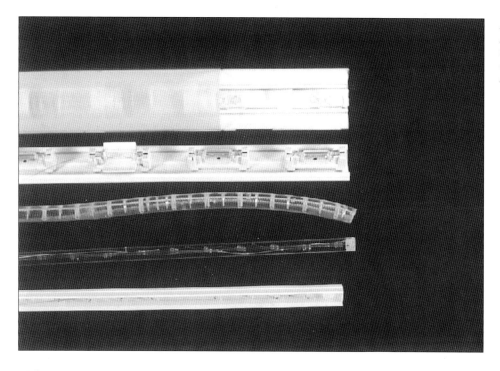

Figure 7.7
Linear strip lighting examples with accessories.
(Photographer: Andrew M. Mitchell, FPI)

Voltages: 120, 12, 24

The products are small in size and can be easily concealed in cabinetry and architectural features.

Common usage: The most common usage for these strip lights are: in ceiling coves or moldings (for even, indirect lighting); under cabinet applications (for illuminating counter tops); interior cabinet lighting; bookcase shelf lighting; wine rack back lighting; stair lighting (concealed under the tread); and, top of cabinet lighting.

Placement: Placement of these products depends on the task at hand. It is important to review the manufacturer catalogs for specific tasks, electrical requirements, code issues and size. The majority of these products require a remote transformer which necessitates calculating the length and the number of lamps per foot. This calculation is critical in design and installation to avoid any voltage drop issues or potential electrical hazards. The 120 volt product is much larger in size and requires a greater scale in the architectural features to conceal the source.

4) Recessed floor or in ground well lights

Description: The recessed floor or in ground well lights are installed flush with the top surface of the receiving medium.

Figure 7.8
Recessed well light samples.
(Photographer:
Andrew M. Mitchell, FPI)

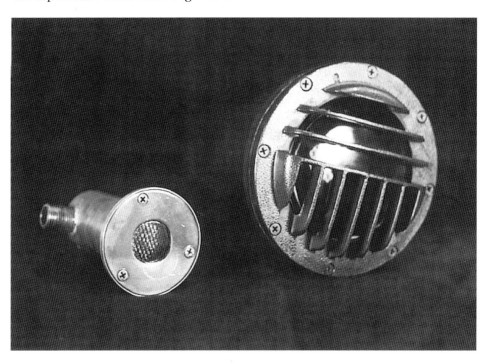

Voltages: 120, 12

These products are intended to disappear as much as possible in the ground or floor. The focus and noticeable effect is the up lit illumination of the targeted object.

Common usage: These products are used mostly as architectural accent lights. They are designed in the base of columns, in floors to illuminate arches or doorways, in rotunda spaces to accent walls, in floors of architectural niches, or in bases of sculptural shelves or niches. These same applications are true in the landscape lighting arena for uplighting trees, sculpture gardens, gazebos, arches, pass through areas and water features. Water exposure sites and other types of vulnerable locations should be identified in the process. Caution must be taken to prevent moisture infiltration of fixture interiors. The lighting designer should specify wet labeled fixtures when they are located in such areas and the installer needs to be aware of proper sealing and maintenance techniques.

Placement: The desired effects should be tested in a similar application. Perform the test prior to the specification of the product and its exact location, especially when the product is in a poured concrete application or other unforgiving surface. It is very difficult and costly to move installed products. Mock-ups are especially effective for this application.

5) Surface mounted lights

Description: Any non-recessed lighting fixture fits into this category. Surface mounting means the product is directly attached to walls, ceilings, or floors.

Common usage: Common products include wall mounted uplights or downlights, pendant area lights, cable systems, address markers, step lighting, and drums.

(a)

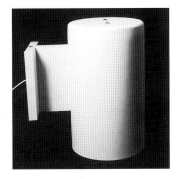

(b)

Figure 7.9
(a) Custom MR11 up/downlight sample.
(b)Wall light cylinder sample.
(c)Pendant sample.
(d)Cable light sample.
(e)Drum sample.
(Photographer: Andrew M. Mitchell, FPI)

(c)

(d)

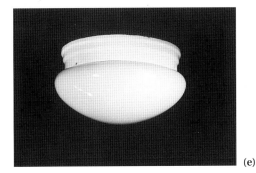

(e)

Voltages: 120, 12, 24

Placement: These fixtures are surface mounted out of necessity due to their inability to recess into the architecture. Surface mounts would be applicable on concrete walls or ceilings, in structural steel impact situations, and in no recessed depth conditions.

6) Track lights

Description: The track light is a surface and/or recessed raceway that accommodates adjustable individual track heads.

Common usage: The track light is most often used for accent lighting of artwork, sculpture, furniture and some area lighting.

Figure 7.10
Track head samples.
(Photographer:
Andrew M. Mitchell, FPI)

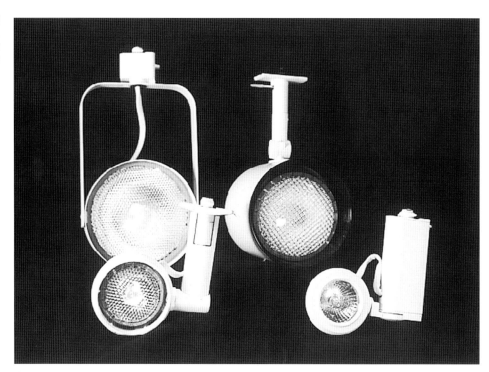

Voltages: 120, 12

Placement: Track lights are appropriate wherever recessed accent lighting cannot be utilized due to structural constraints and where flexibility is needed. It is important to use the manufacturers' guidelines for distance which are based on ceiling mounting height and the objects being illuminated in the space (see Chapter Fifteen). Placing the lights too close to the wall will distract from the object, and the same is true in placement of recessed accent lights.

CHAPTER EIGHT

Lamps

The most important element of the fixture is the lamp selected for the task. The finished appearance of the product on the ceiling is usually the determining selection factor with recessed lighting products. Fixture performance is not always crucial because it is often the selected lamp that fulfills the desired criteria. In particular, PAR (parabolic aluminized reflector) lamps and MR (multi-reflector) low-voltage lamps provide their own built-in reflector to project illumination.

Figure 8.1
PAR30 and MR16 lamps.
(Photographer:
Andrew M. Mitchell, FPI)

Consequently, a fixture's illumination performance is only limited by the aperture size and lamp's adjustability.

The most commonly used lamps available for contemporary residences fall into five main categories:
Incandescent, Halogen, Fluorescent, Compact Fluorescent and Xenon (show lamps and various sizes).

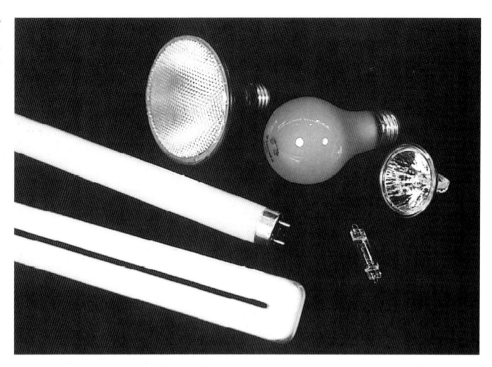

The information for each lamp includes the size, beam spread, and wattage utilized most often in residences. Note: the number designation listed in the lamp size indicates the bulb's maximum diameter. Divide the number by eight to determine the size in inches, unless otherwise noted. For example, a bulb designated as A 21 has a maximum diameter of 2 1/8 or 2 5/8 inches.

Incandescent lamps are the most commonplace light source. Light and heat are produced as electric current passes through a thin wire filament (usually tungsten). Incandescent lamps offer low initial cost, versatility, and excellent color rendering qualities. This 120 volt source is operable over a wide range of ambient temperatures, is easily dimmed, and turns on instantly. Disadvantages include low efficiency, short life, and high heat output. The following are the most typically utilized incandescent lamps.

A LAMP (STANDARD)

Description: This lamp is the common light bulb and it is available in clear, frosted and colored finishes.

Figure 8.3
Common A lamp samples:
A15, A17, A19 and A21.
(Photographer:
Andrew M. Mitchell, FPI)

This source radiates light in all directions.

Beam spreads: not applicable
Life span: up to 2500 hours = 1.36 years of standard use (5 hours/day)
Sizes: A15, A17, A19, A21, A23
Wattage: 15 (A15) - 250 (A23)
Usage in fixture categories: 1, 4, 5, 6
Accessories: not applicable

R LAMP (REFLECTOR)

Description: The lamp has an interior aluminized reflector that projects light, rather than radiates light.

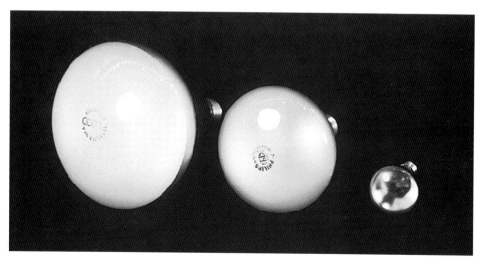

Figure 8.4
Common R lamp samples: R40,
R30 and R14.
(Photographer:
Andrew M. Mitchell, FPI)

It produces a soft glow of illumination. It is a good area or wall wash source, but not effective for accent lighting. Government legislation has begun to phase out the older R lamp, however it is still commonly used in outdoor protected flood lights and recessed downlights. Lamp manufacturers have begun to utilize halogen gas technology with this lamp to improve efficiency.

Beam spreads: spot, medium flood, flood - availability varies between manufacturers and model numbers

Figure 8.5
R Lamp distribution.

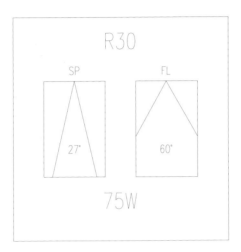
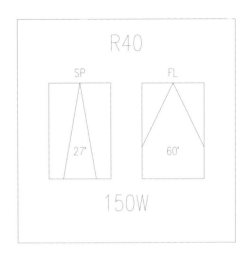

Life span: 2,000 hours = 1.09 years of standard use (5 hours/day)
Sizes: R14, R20, R30, R40
Wattage: 25 (R14) - 250 (R40)
Usage in Fixture Categories: 1, 4, 5, 6
Accessories: Honeycomb baffles can be used in downlight and well light applications to aid in glare reduction.

Halogen or tungsten halogen lamps house halogen gas inside a quartz glass bulb. This gas burns at a high temperature to produce a very bright light. The tungsten filament in incandescent sources burns and accumulates on the glass bulb, thereby reducing light output and shortening the lamp life. In halogen lamps, the gas keeps the tungsten from accumulating on the glass (it redistributes it to the filament) which increases light output and lamp life. The color rendering properties of halogen lamps are very high. The initial cost is often higher than that of incandescent lamps, but the energy saved over time and the extended lamp life is well worth the investment. Halogen lamps are available in 12, 120, and 130 volt. The 12 volt lamps are smaller and have excellent beam control. The 130 volt lamps can be used in 120 volt applications to double lamp life, with minor light reduction. It should be noted that these halogen sources produce high levels of heat which are accounted for in most manufacturers' fixtures.

PAR Lamp (Parabolic Aluminized Reflector)

Description: This lamp is utilized indoors/outdoors, and is also available as incandescent. New technology such as halogen infra-red has made this lamp extremely efficient.

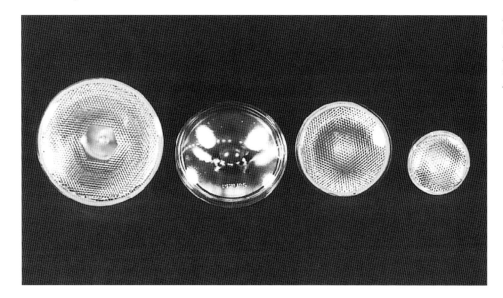

Figure 8.6
Common PAR lamp samples:
PAR38, PAR36, PAR30 and
PAR20.
(Photographer:
Andrew M. Mitchell, FPI)

With most incandescent lamps, the electric current heats the tungsten filament and, as a result, visible light and infra-red radiation are emitted and energy is wasted in the process. This lamp avoids waste with a film that reflects the infra-red radiation back onto the filament, thereby reducing heat and energy use. For example, a 60 watt halogen infra-red PAR produces the equivalent light to a standard 150 watt PAR.

Beam spreads: very narrow spot, narrow spot, spot, narrow flood, flood, wide flood

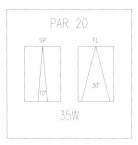

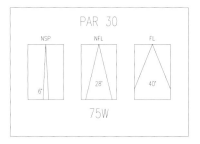

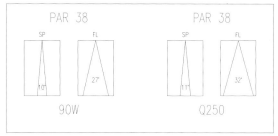

Figure 8.7
PAR lamp distribution.

Life span: up to 6,000 hours = 3.28 years of standard use (5 hours/day)
Sizes: PAR20, PAR30, PAR38 (120 and 130 volt), PAR36 (12 volt)
Wattage: 35-250
Usage in fixture categories: 1, 4, 5, 6
Accessories: Honeycomb baffles can be used in downlight and well light applications to aid in glare reduction.

MR LAMP (MULTI-REFLECTOR)

Description: This small, powerful 12 or 24 volt lamp has excellent beam control and is often utilized as an accent for art and sculpture.

*Figure 8.8
MR16 and MR11 lamps.
(Photographer:
Andrew M. Mitchell, FPI)*

It is critical to use the higher quality lamps with special coatings, because inferior lamps have colored light output, instead of a desirable white light. The MR lamp has allowed fixtures to have much smaller apertures and has revolutionized lighting design.

Beam spreads: very narrow spot, narrow spot, spot, narrow flood, flood, wide flood, very wide flood

*Figure 8.9
MR16 and MR11 lamp
distributions.*

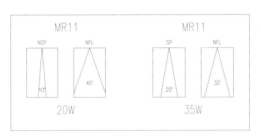

Life span: 4000 - 5000 hours = 2.17 to 2.73 years of standard use (5 hours/day)
Sizes: MR11, MR16
Wattage: 20-75
Usage in fixture categories: 2, 3, 4, 5, 6
Accessories: clear, frosted or colored lenses; honeycomb louvers

AR Lamp (Aluminum Reflector)

Description: This low-voltage (6v and 12v) lamp allows for excellent beam control, even from high ceilings.

Figure 8.10
Common AR lamp samples:
AR48 and AR70.
(Photographer:
Andrew M. Mitchell, FPI)

It is only available from Osram Sylvania.

Beam spreads: super spot, spot, flood

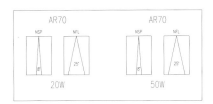
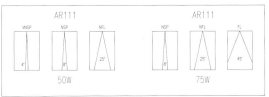

Figure 8.11
AR lamp distributions.

Life span: 2000 hours = 1.09 years of standard use (5 hours/day)
Sizes: AR48, AR70, AR111 (note: these lamps are measured in mm, not inches as described above)
Wattage: 20-75
Usage in fixture categories: 1, 2, 4, 5, 6
Accessories: honeycomb louver

A **fluorescent lamp** is comprised of a glass tube that has an internal coating of phosphor. Phosphors give off light, or fluoresce, when activated by ultraviolet radiation. The type of phosphor in the tube determines the color of light given off. Less expensive lamps have poor color rendering properties, while more expensive tubes, with rare phosphors, have a higher CRI. These lamps are generally quite efficient for the low amount of consumed energy. Fluorescent lamps offer moderate initial cost and long life, but require special low temperature starting ballasts (when temperature is below 50 degrees). Dimming ballasts are available at a substantial cost addition.

TUBE FLUORESCENT LAMPS

Description: The fluorescent tube is what fills many kitchens and garages with diffuse, bright light.

Figure 8.12
Common fluorescent lamp samples: T2, T5, T8 and T12.
(Photographer:
Andrew M. Mitchell, FPI)

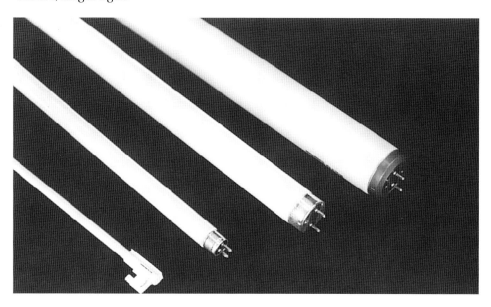

Tubes are available in rapid start (most common), instant start and preheat types. The lengths and widths vary, as do the shape: straight tube, U-shaped, and circular-shaped tubes are available.

Beam spreads: n/a
Life span: 8,000 (preheat) to 20,000 (rapid start) hours = 2.73 to 6.84 years of standard use (3 hours/start & 5 hours/day)
Sizes: T2, T5, T8, T12
Wattage: 4 - 110
Usage in categories: 5
Accessories: n/a

Compact fluorescent lamps are the latest trend in fluorescent technology. These small lamps are very efficient.

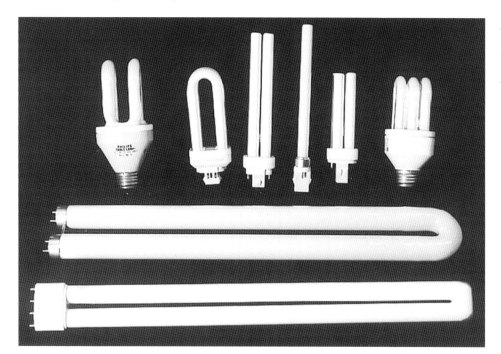

Figure 8.13
Various compact fluorescent
lamp samples.
(Photographer: Andrew M.
Mitchell, FPI)

They produce as many lumens at one-fourth the watts as standard incandescent lamps. They are often required by codes in many areas for retrofits and new construction. The compact fluorescent lamp has a folded configuration which allows a much higher light output than the standard linear tube fluorescent.

Description: Common configurations include twin tube, quad tube, and six tube among others. Note that there is a lot of variation between manufacturers' lamps, and most are not interchangeable.

Beam spreads n/a
Life span: 9,000 to 10,000 hours = 3.08 to 3.42 years of standard use (3 hours/start & 5 hours/day)
Wattage: 10-50
Usage in fixture categories: 1, 5
Accessories: n/a

Xenon lamps are small (two inch) glass tubes filled with xenon gas.

*Figure 8.14
Xenon lamp samples.
(Photographer: Andrew M.
Mitchell, FPI)*

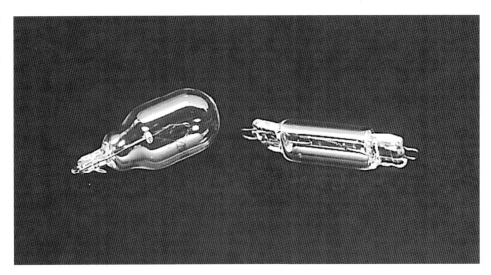

These 24 volt lamps burn very bright and produce a white light perfectly suited for cove/indirect lighting applications. Their low profile allows for under-cabinet installations.

Beam spreads: n/a
Life span: 5,000 to 10,000 hours (depending on wattage) = 2.73 to 5.47 years of standard use (5 hours/day)
Sizes: T3 1/4, T5
Wattage: 5 - 10
Usage in fixture categories: 3
Accessories: reflectors, lens covers, frosted lamps

Lamp technology is changing rapidly — the emphasis is on excellent color rendering, extended lamp life and energy efficiency. It is critical that lighting designers remain current on these improvements and quickly implement the changes into their lighting designs. The most effective way for the lighting designer to stay on top of these changes is to become involved and informed about the industry. Attendance at various lighting seminars and manufacturers' presentations and subscriptions to trade publications are particularly beneficial (see Resource Appendix).

CHAPTER NINE

The Lighting Control System

Lighting control design is as critical as the lighting design itself. A lighting consultant can design a wonderful artistic atmosphere for the home, but miss the mark completely by neglecting the lighting control. In today's sophisticated residences, it is no longer acceptable to clutter walls with rows of switches which detract from the architecture and interior design.

Figure 9.1
(a) Wall clutter.

(b)Consolidate controls.
(Carm and Nancy
Santoro Residence)
(Photographer:
Andrew M. Mitchell, FPI)

The owners become frustrated when they have to guess which switch controls a group of lights.

The process of selecting a control system can be overwhelming for the homeowners. The lighting designer often recommends and designs the lighting control system based on information obtained from the homeowners. The following questionnaire can help distinguish the owners' priorities.

Questions to determine when to use a lighting control system.
What is the:

> Budget ? (First and Foremost.)
> Client needs/requests?
> Client familiarity with electronics?
> Size of the home?
> Use of the home? (main home or vacation or entertainment home.)

Questions regarding function.
How does the client feel about:

> Global home control ? (On/off, Home, Away buttons.)
> Pathway control buttons? (Master bedroom to bathroom, kitchen, children's room, etc.)
> Security through lighting system? (Panic button locations.)
> Ease of use?
> Vacation modes? (Away button.)
> Integration with other systems? (audio/video, heating and air conditioning, security.)
> Telephone/Modem interface? (Use from car or other remote phone sites.)
> Ability to expand the system through programming vs. re-wiring?

The audio/video consultant will usually be responsible for the control system selection and design if the lighting designer does not include lighting control in his or her services. Why the audio/video consultant? The lighting control manufacturers realized that if a particular lighting designer was not sophisticated enough to design an elaborate lighting control system (and the electrical contractor was not called in soon enough) it would be necessary to have another consultant market their product. The obvious choice was the audio/video consultant, who deals with high dollar, sophisticated, low-voltage wiring systems and components. Manufacturers may sign the A/V consultants as dealers or distributors of dimming systems, however there are financial considerations. The electrical contractor and wholesale distributor, in some cases, are bypassed completely . Instead of working as a team, they are now competitors, and the A/V consultant becomes an enemy to the electrical contractor. For this reason, it is more professional to find a non-supplying lighting designer, who includes the specification and design of the lighting control system in their services. Ultimately, it is best for the electrical contractor to purchase these high priced systems through normal distribution channels, such as financially strong electrical wholesale supply houses.

THE SELECTION PROCESS:

There are actually only five lighting control systems widely used in the market today. They are the following:

1) The standard wall switch and wall box dimmer.
2) PLC or Power Line Carrier devices for switching and limited dimming.
3) Self Contained Programmable Units
4) Centralized Processing Systems
5) Distributed Processing Systems

The Standard Wall Switch and Wall Box Dimmer

Most homeowners are familiar with these devices.

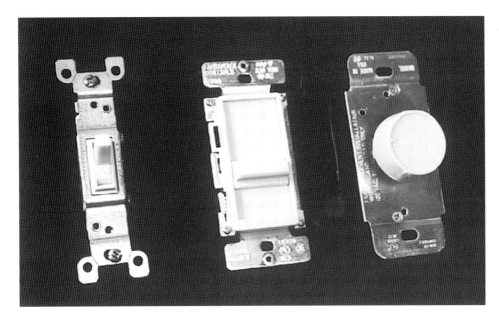

Figure 9.2
Standard switch, slide dimmer and rotary dimmer.
(Photographer: Andrew M. Mitchell, FPI)

Chapter Two describes how wall dimmers soften the glaring effects of grid lighting. Early wall box dimmers for incandescent sources had limited wattage capabilities of only 600 watts. Today, lower cost wall box dimmers are available for incandescent, fluorescent and low-voltage lighting sources with the ability to handle 1000 watt loads.

Advantages	Disadvantages
Easy installation	Limited function
Easily retrofit into existing structures	Audible feedback from dimmer
and lamps Minimal cost	Not very attractive

PLC or Power Line Carrier Devices for Switching and Limited Dimming

These devices carry data signals over conventional wiring to electrical plug-in modules. The usual configuration is a lamp plugged into the module, which is then plugged into the wall outlet.

Figure 9.3
(a) Table top control device.
(b)Programmable receptacle.
(Courtesy of X10)

(a)

(b)

The module is dialed in to coincide with a table top controller that is also plugged into an outlet. Pressing a button on the table top controller allows the data signal to be carried over the conventional house wiring (instructing the lamp module to activate).

Advantages	Disadvantages
Good for adding convenience to existing home	Some electrical interference
	Phasing problems
Low cost	Incompatible with some devices
Relatively easy to install	

Self Contained Programmable Units

These hardwired devices offer dimming, limited scene function, and multiple switching capabilities through preset stations.

Figure 9.4
Self contained
programmable units.
(Photographer:
Andrew M. Mitchell, FPI)

Advantages	Disadvantages
Good retrofit devices	Limited load definition
Easy installation	Audible feedback when dimming
User friendly programming	Commercial appearance
Minimal cost	Devices take up wall space

Centralized Processing Systems

One micro-processor handles the communication between lighting control key-pads, modules (relays or dimmers), and loads (lights, motors, switched outlets).

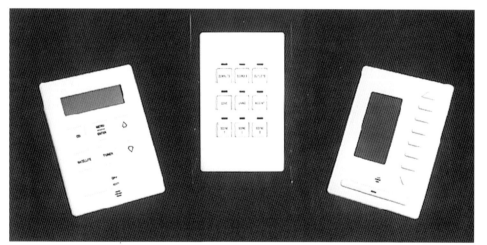

Figure 9.5
Centralized control devices.
(Photographer:
Andrew M. Mitchell, FPI)

Modern micro-processors seldom collapse the system. Failures are usually due to other communication drivers or installation problems. Always verify integration compatibility and past performance records on peripheral devices.

Advantages

Easier troubleshooting

Lower cost on larger projects

Fewer components to fail

Disadvantages

In the event of complete processor

Failure, the entire system may go down

Distributed Processing Systems

Several micro-processors are spread throughout the control system and are tied together. They are usually housed in each enclosure (or a series of enclosures) and there is intelligence in each lighting control keypad.

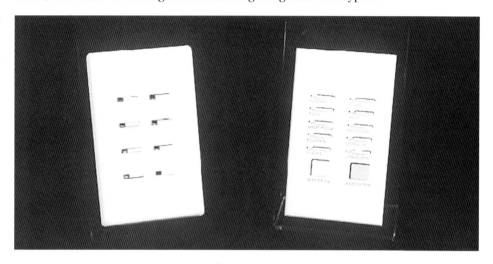

Figure 9.6
Distributed control devices.
(Photographer:
Andrew M. Mitchell, FPI)

Each micro-processor handles the communication of a small group of keypads and loads resident to its enclosures.

Advantages

When a single processor fails, only the loads tied into the enclosure are affected

All other enclosures and loads will remain in operation

Disadvantages

More processors equal more costs

More time spent troubleshooting potential problems

As mentioned before, the first introduction to lighting control usually comes through the lighting consultant. It is very important that the lighting consultant remain monetarily independent from the lighting control systems. An experienced lighting designer should represent the clients' best interests, given the overwhelming nature of the various products on the market. All of the lighting manufacturers, dealers, distributors and representatives will tell the client that their product is far superior to the others. Of course, this is their job, but in most instances these individuals do not completely understand the client's needs, wants, and wishes regarding the lighting design and lighting control system. It is ultimately the lighting designer's responsibility to determine the specification, based upon the owners' needs and budgets. The specification should not be based on the sales pitch of a manufacturer, distributor, dealer, or representative.

Part 4

Residential Illumination Techniques

CHAPTER TEN

Entry Illumination Techniques

The entry, including the exterior porte-cochere, creates a memorable impression of the home. The approach to lighting design for these areas is artistic and functional with a balance of decorative, indirect and accent lighting. Good general illumination is also taken into consideration.

The following lighting requirements for the entry are:
- Medium area lighting levels throughout entry and porte-cochere
- Dramatic architectural illumination
- Dramatic accent lighting on art, furnishings or other features
- Incorporation of exterior lighting effects of porte-cochere
- Scene pre-set lighting control
- Sufficient illumination to safely reveal hazards, such as steps and ice

Figure 10.1
Potential details for entry
illumination techniques:
(a) column downlights,
(b) low voltage cove lighting,
(c) column uplights in column
base, (d) walk light,
(e) wall mount adjustable
uplight,
(f) low voltage lighting in beam,
(g) fluorescent biax uplight.

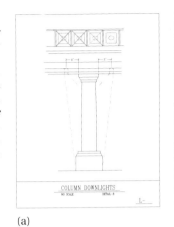

(a)

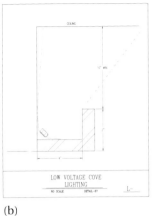

(b)

(c)

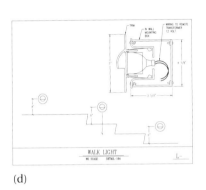

(d)

(e)

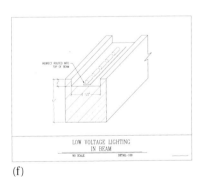

(f)

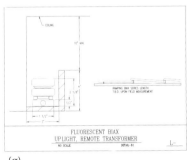

(g)

Figure 10.2
This mountain top entry is a
perfect example of architectural
lighting. With the addition of the
ceiling cove molding in the
lighting design process and the
custom designed mini-well
lights, the space comes alive.
In addition to the architectural
lighting added elements of stair
illumination, decorative fixtures
and art accent lighting round out
this beautiful entry.
(Karen and Richard
Gomez Residence)
(Photographer:
Andrew M. Mitchell, FPI)

Figure 10.3
This Beverly Hills Classic style
entry comes alive by introducing
hidden, subtle exterior
uplighting on the building,as
well as in the fountain and
planting area. Additional accent
lighting was placed on the trees,
furthering the dimension and
drama. The entry wall sconces tie
into the style of the home and
add additional ambiance to the
greeting area. The door is also
strategically illuminated by a
pin-hole downlight which grazes
the old world carved specimen.
(Photographer: Grey Crawford)

Figure 10.4
This refined rustic style home was illuminated by the lighting designer's added cove details, which define the architectural ceilings, contribute volume to the space and give a warm feeling to this entry. In addition, area accent lighting is placed to illuminate the entry upper landing and the stairs for safety and aesthetics. Wall sconces were placed flanking the entry with an additional pendant fixture to add decoration to the greeting area. The painting is illuminated with a concealed optical framing projector from the high ceiling. (Photographer: Andrew M. Mitchell, FPI)

Figure 10.5
The snow covered resort home utilizes many lighting details for its beauty. The lighting designer suggested the combination cove and uplights to dramatically offset this entry. Along with the tree lighting, eave lighting and the decorative sconces, this entry is a show stopper. (Photographer: Andrew M. Mitchell, FPI)

Figure 10.6
This south-western Las Vegas entry porte-cochere boasts a beautiful acrylic barrel ceiling held up by statuesque columns which come to life with the lighting designer's added details. In addition, fiber optic uplit water features flanking the entry path and exterior track lighting enhances the low level planting below.
(Carole and Jerry Turk Las Vegas Residence)
(Photographer: Chawla Photography)

Figure 10.7
The welcome mat rolls out as guests approach this wonderful home with the warm glow from the decorative lanterns and eave accent lighting located by the lighting designer. In addition, landscape lighting accents the trees and grazes the two story stone front. The front door is illuminated by eave accent lights.
(Photographer: Andrew M. Mitchell, FPI)

Figure 10.8
This Rocky Mountain retreat's
entry is a piece of art itself.
The massive thematic chandelier
welcomes visitors as soon as
they cross the threshold.
The additional art accents
highlighting the Indian artifacts
and sculpture creates the mood
for the rest of the home's
wonderful experience.
(Photographer:
Andrew M. Mitchell, FPI)

Figure 10.9
This log structure entry brings
visitors back to the basics as they
approach. Through strategically
placed uplights on each log
column, decorative hanging
lanterns and exterior eave lights
the lighting designer adds
warmth, charm and character.
Exterior moon lighting fixtures in
the trees add to the ambiance.
(Photographer:
Andrew M. Mitchell, FPI)

CHAPTER ELEVEN

Living, Family and Great Room Illumination Techniques

The living, family and great room areas contain the most dramatic illumination. These rooms incorporate the finest furniture, art work and architectural detailing because they are used for entertaining. It is the lighting designer's responsibility to highlight and accent these items, and create a breathtaking ambiance.

The following lighting requirements are necessary for the living, family and great rooms:

- Medium overall light level
- Specific accent lighting on art, furniture and other accessories
- Dramatic architectural illumination
- Strategically placed sconces, chandeliers, table and floor lamps
- Scene pre-set lighting control
- Maximized view areas through exterior lighting
- Avoidance of ambient sound from fixtures, transformers, and dimmed lamps
- Minimal high ceiling lamp maintenance
- Control of ultra-violet output to preserve artwork

Figure 11.1
Potential details for living, family, and great room illumination techniques: (a) low voltage lighting in beam, (b) fluorescent biax uplight, (c) PAR38, (d) recessed outlets in mantel, (e) fixed wall uplight, (f) wall mount adjustable uplight, (g) low voltage shelf lights (h) strip switch (i) recessed strip light in mantel.

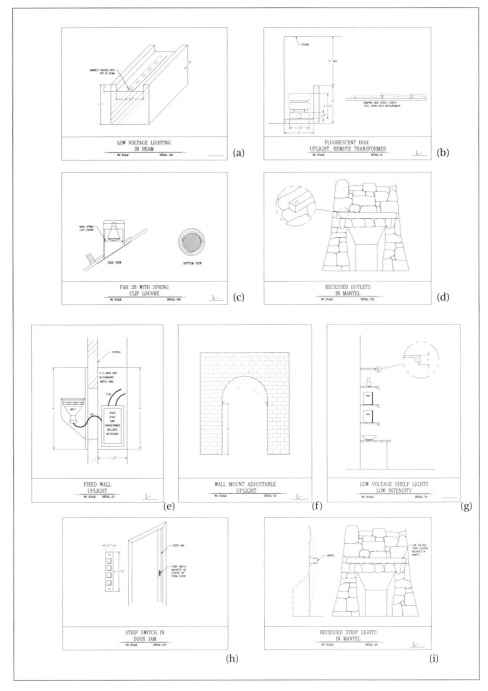

Figure 11.2
This southern California beach home presented unusual challenges due to its construction: concrete! All recessed lighting fixtures needed to be poured in place, with the exception of a few drop ceiling locations. In the process, the lighting designer soon realized the lack of concrete-pour lighting products offered by manufacturers. Low-voltage exterior landscape lighting fixtures were modified for ceiling use and U.L. labeled accordingly. Additional conditions such as salt air added to the difficulty in that most of the lighting fixtures needed to be sealed. Cove lighting was added within recessed troughs in the concrete designed by the lighting designer. The final effects are subtle and dramatic with the maximizing of the views being paramount; exterior eave lighting draws the viewer's eye through the glass.
(Photographer: Mary E. Nichols)

Figure 11.3
This cozy sitting room is illuminated exclusively by low-voltage accent and area lighting. The addition of the large beams added to the ceiling helped to virtually conceal the actual lighting sources.
(Photographer:
Andrew M. Mitchell, FPI)

Figure 11.4
This refined Rocky Mountain
guest home was a retrofit by the
lighting designer with art accent
lights (optical framing projector
on the painting) and the proper
lamps (located in the beams
above; not shown in the photo)
to perform the tasks of
washing the fireplace, as well as
accenting the coffee table and
conversation area.
(Photographer:
Andrew M. Mitchell, FPI)

Figure 11.5
This whimsical interior incorpo-
rated custom designed lighting
fixtures by the interior designer
(over dining table) and commis-
sioned art in the form of Alice in
Wonderland. Dramatic lighting
scenes were created to add to the
stage like setting of this home.
Low-voltage accent lighting,
optical framing projectors on the
mural, wall sconces for ceiling
uplighting and decorative lamps
all add to the experience.
(Photographer:
Andrew M. Mitchell, FPI)

Figure 11.6
This casual sitting room incorporates lamp light in conjunction with recessed low-voltage ceiling lights which accent the bookcases, art over fire place, sofa back table and interior plants. These aspects contribute a cozy feeling without detracting from the 9 foot ceiling heights. (Karen and Richard Gomez Residence)
(Photographer: Andrew M. Mitchell, FPI)

Figure 11.7
Indirect cove lighting, small aperture ceiling accents highlighting sculpture and furnishings and added decorative lighting create an inviting atmosphere in this large and potentially impersonal room.
(Photographer: Andrew M. Mitchell, FPI)

Figure 11.8
(a) Computer elevation
illustrating lighting techniques.

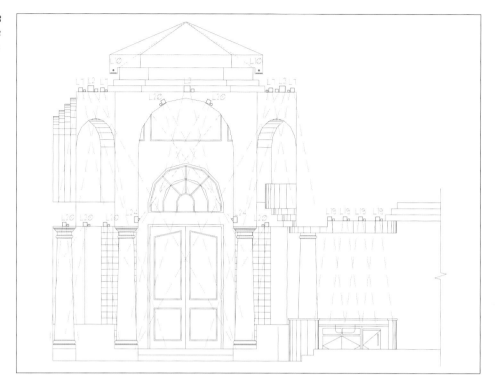

(b) Many lighting details are
incorporated into this Las Vegas
home. With the addition of col-
umn accent lights, interior arch
lighting, cove lighting, art accent
lighting, area lighting and view
lighting in the exterior eaves not
an element was missed.
(Carole and Jerry Turk
Las Vegas Residence)
(Photographer:
Chawla Photography)

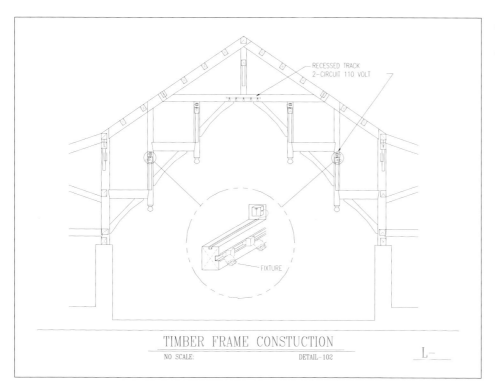

Figure 11.9
(a) Computer elevation illustrating lighting techniques.

(b) This timber frame structure held many challenges that were expertly resolved. Through routing out framing members, the lighting designer created hidden indirect lighting pockets to beautifully illuminate the cherry wood ceilings. Also recessed tracks were incorporated into the side of beams concealing the art accent lights highlighting tapestries, grind stone over the fireplace and the furniture below. (Photographer: Andrew M. Mitchell, FPI)

Figure 11.10
Various scene settings are
available with the touch
of a button:
(a) Scene 1, (b) Scene 2
(c) Scene 3.
(Video clip by
Andrew M. Mitchell, FPI)

(a)

(b)

(c)

Dining Room Illumination Techniques

The dining room is an area that screams for drama and excitement. Most formal dining room are filled with wonderful furniture and art pieces. The experience in this space, through lighting, should be with the elegance of a favorite restaurant and the simplicity of really being able to see what you are eating. A good balance of decorative, task and artwork illumination are in order.

The following lighting requirements for the dining room are:
* Direct table illumination from accent lighting
* Combination of decorative wall sconces and chandelier
* Art accent lighting
* Interior cabinet lighting

Figure 12.1
Potential details for dining room
illumination techniques:
(a) interior cabinet lighting,
(b) linear cabinet lighting,
(c) linear lighting routed in shelf,
(d) recessed outlets in mantel,
(e) low voltage cove lighting,
(f) low voltage shelf lights
(g) wine rack illumination,
(h) display case fiber
optic lighting.

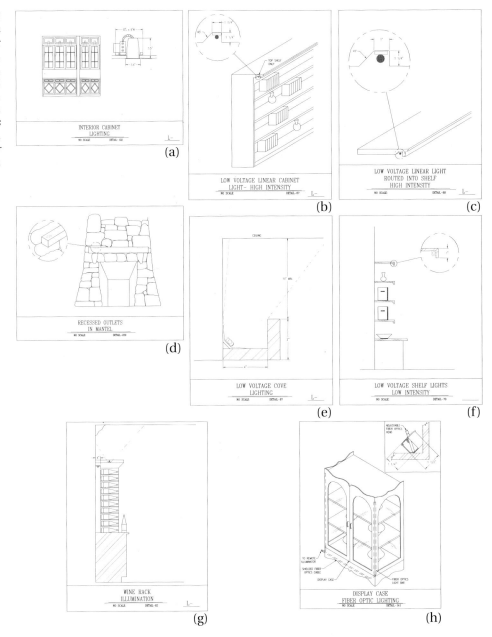

Figure 12.2
The focal point of this dining room is the custom made chandelier designed by the interior designer. Additional lighting incorporated is the recessed low-voltage accent lighting on the carved corner columns and interior china cabinet lighting. Also exterior eave lighting and snow scene lighting were added to the lower roof line.
(Photographer: Andrew M. Mitchell, FPI)

Figure 12.3
This elegant dining room incorporates the traditional chandelier along with separately controlled low-voltage table accent lights and art and wall lighting. Two wax candle sconces add a decorative element.
(Photographer: Andrew M. Mitchell, FPI)

Figure 12.4
This intimate dining area
created in a massive volume of
space works due to the built-in
buffet that separates the dining
from the living space. Also with
this challenge the lighting
designer brought down the sense
of scale by lowering a chandelier
to normal height, adding the dec-
orative wall sconces flanking the
interior illuminated china cabi-
net and specifying low-voltage
fixtures in the high ceiling to
accent the table top. This all
makes for a very comfortable
dining environment.
(Photographer:
Andrew M. Mitchell, FPI)

Figure 12.5
This eat-in dining room depicts
the importance of adding table
accent lighting to illuminate
flower arrangements in a non-
eating setting. In a dining setting
the china, flatware and table
decorations will come to life
adding another dimension to the
decorative chandelier and fire-
place accent light.
(Karen and Richard
Gomez Residence)
(Photographer:
Andrew M. Mitchell, FPI)

Figure 12.6
The selection of the decorative lighting fixtures are critical to the success of the space. Even though they are largely props added to the architecture through the artistic talent of the interior designer, space is created with these items. Low-voltage art accent lighting adds to the drama of the art and high intensity indirect decorative fixtures illuminate the volume of the ceiling above.
(Karen and Richard Gomez Residence)
(Photographer: Andrew M. Mitchell, FPI)

Figure 12.7
This Las Vegas masterpiece held many challenges for the lighting designer. The owner requested adequate table illumination without dropping a decorative fixture for the high ceiling. He also wanted his crystal sculpture to come alive with brilliance through lighting. Low-voltage high intensity products were successfully selected for the task. Art accent lighting, cabinet lighting and subtle area lighting rounded out this wonderful lighting design.
(Photographer: Chawla Photography)

CHAPTER THIRTEEN:

Kitchen Illumination Techniques

The kitchen and bathroom areas of the home are perhaps the most important and difficult rooms to illuminate. Efficient lighting is imperative in these rooms because of their utilitarian functions.

The following lighting requirements are necessary for the kitchen:
- High overall lighting level
- Non-glaring task lighting on counters, sink and preparation areas
- Interior cabinet illumination
- Interior hood lighting over cook top
- Multi-level lighting control capabilities

Figure 13.1
Potential details for kitchen illu-
mination techniques:
(a) low voltage lighting in beam,
(b) interior cabinet lighting,
(c) downlights in cabinet,
(d) linear cabinet lighting,
(e) lighting under bar
and countertop,
(f) wine rack illumination,
(g) top / under cabinet lighting
(h) under cabinet lighting.

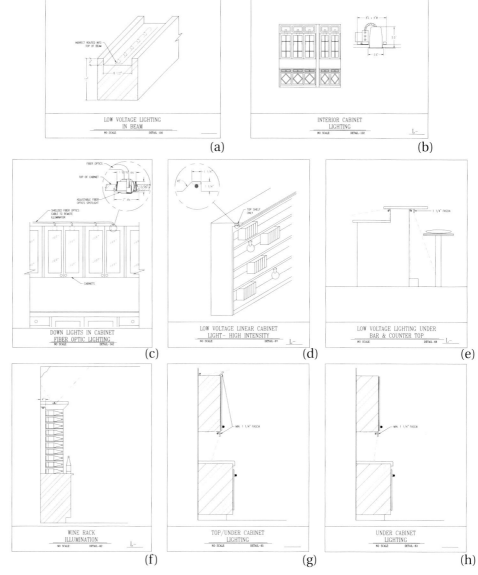

(a)

(b)

(c)

(d)

(e)

(f)

(g)

(h)

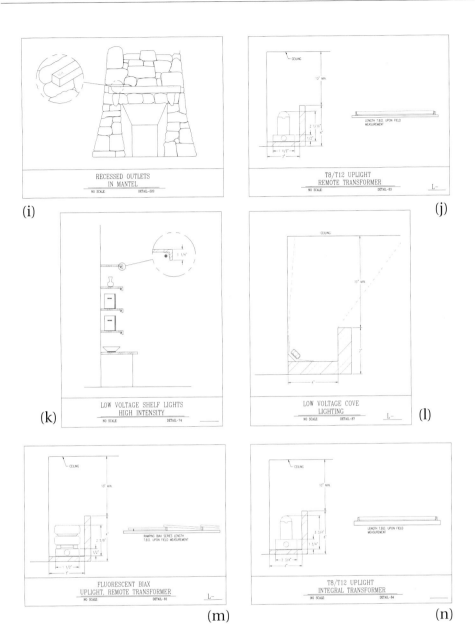

Figure 13.2
Potential details for kitchen illumination techniques continued:
(i) recessed outlets in mantel,
(j) fluorescent uplight,
remote transformer
(k) shelf lighting,
(l) low voltage cove lighting,
(m) biax uplight, remote
transformer
(n) fluorescent uplight integral
transformer.

Figure 13.3
This kitchen incorporates the necessary illumination levels to successfully operate in. Excellent task lighting directly over the preparation island,counter space and sink allows for a great working environment. Hood lighting not activated in this photo also allows for good cooking light.
(Karen and Richard Gomez Residence)
(Photographer: Andrew M. Mitchell, FPI)

Figure 13.4
This home's kitchen is commercial in nature and also falls into California's Title 24 energy rules making fluorescent lighting the integral source. High intensity island lighting through low-voltage pin-hole lights, fluorescent direct lighting behind the coffered ceiling, high intensity under cabinet lighting, area lighting and hood lighting add to the success of this kitchen.
(Photographer: Andrew M. Mitchell, FPI)

Figure 13.5
Kitchen cabinet designs and details are essential for the success of the implementing the lighting design. When this information is available early in the process, the lighting design can provide for top of cabinet illumination and under cabinet illumination. Low-voltage task lighting was added to the bar top, island and wall accent lights behind the eat in kitchen table. Decorative lighting fixtures and recessed area lights add to the overall general illumination. (Photographer: Andrew M. Mitchell, FPI)

Figure 13.6
This southern California home posed a significant challenge to the lighting designer. The challenge was to provide illumination from the high ceilings without dropping any product from the ceiling. The suggestion by the lighting designer was to box in the beams above and incorporate high intensity downlighting and indirect lighting for effect. The final effects were excellent task lighting levels on the island from the lighting above as well as an artistic ambiance with the indirect beam illumination. Also interior cabinet lighting, under cabinet lighting and lower soffit lighting were added to supplement the lighting above. Success, success, success!! (Photographer: Mary E. Nichols)

Figure 13.7
This contemporary kitchen is a
beautiful work of art. Where
would it be without well planned
lighting? Indirect top of cabinet
lighting, high intensity under
cabinet lighting, task lighting on
the island, hood lighting and
general area lighting help create
this functional masterpiece.
(Dan and Kim Huish Residence)
(Photographer:
Andrew M. Mitchell, FPI)

CHAPTER FOURTEEN

Bedroom Illumination Techniques

The bedroom is also an area for lighting with drama — not just foot candles. Most clients are vague about desired lighting effects in their house. However, when it comes to the bedroom, they know exactly what they want.

The following lighting requirements for the bedroom are:
- Excellent reading ability from the bed
- Dramatic accent lighting on art and furnishings
- Soft and intimate romance lighting
- Placement of wall sconces, chandeliers, floor and bed side lamps
- Scene pre-set, path way and master lighting control ability
- Avoidance of ambient sound from fixtures, transformers, and dimmed lamps

*Figure 14.1
Potential details for bedroom
illumination techniques:
(a) recessed outlets in mantel,
(b) wall mount adjustable
uplight.*

RECESSED OUTLETS
IN MANTEL

NO SCALE: DETAIL-220

(a)

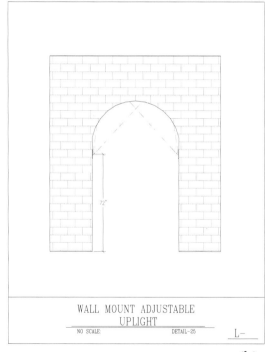

WALL MOUNT ADJUSTABLE
UPLIGHT

NO SCALE: DETAIL-25

(b)

Figure 14.2
This Malibu, California master bedroom with ocean view sitting room is heaven on earth.
By adding an optical framing projector on the painting over the fireplace and small low-voltage area and accent lighting and side table lamps this room speaks comfort and elegance.
(Photographer:
Andrew M. Mitchell, FPI)

Figure 14.3
The decorative ceiling fixtures in this timber frame residence are the jewels of this bedroom. In conjunction with concealed indirect beam illumination, accent lighting on the fireplace and cabinetry and bed side lamps join to make this a welcoming atmosphere.
(Photographer:
Andrew M. Mitchell, FPI)

Figure 14.4
Complete elegance. Clean and simple, low-voltage accent and area lighting with night stand and writing table lamps completes this masterful bedroom. (Karen and Richard Gomez Residence) (Photographer: Andrew M. Mitchell, FPI)

Figure 14.5
Sleeping on the beach will never be the same again. Low-voltage accent lighting, indirect cove lighting and bedside lamps are contained in this seaside treat. (Photographer: Mary E. Nichols)

Figure 14.6
Construction challenges led to the lighting effects in this bedroom. The ceiling was constructed in such a manner that recessing any lighting products would be impossible. The lighting designer's choice was to add the small ceiling uplights into the header between the windows, linear strip uplighting in the top of the fireplace mantel to streak up the rock face, under hearth lighting and picture lights on the art. The decorative lighting joins in to make this bedroom glow with illumination.
(Photographer: Andrew M. Mitchell, FPI)

CHAPTER FIFTEEN:

Bathroom Illumination Techniques

As mentioned earlier, the kitchen and bathroom are by far the most difficult areas to illuminate and are also the most frequented areas in the home. You might ask why is the bathroom difficult to illuminate? A great deal of the time that is spent in the bathroom is for grooming. Proper illumination is critical, but is often neglected in this regard.

The following lighting requirements are necessary for the bathroom:
- High overall lighting levels
- Excellent task lighting for the vanity area
- Excellent color rendering properties
- Sufficient lighting for the tub and shower areas
- Night light feature through lighting control
- Soft and intimate romance lighting ability
- Cove and other indirect lighting

Figure 15.1
Potential details for bathroom
illumination techniques:
(a) soffited Vanitylite,
(b) custom etched glass vanity
light, (c) floating Vanitylite.

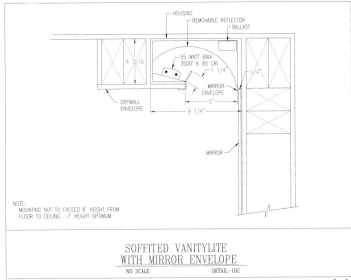

(a)

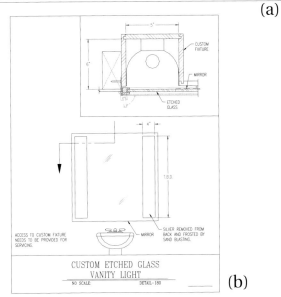

(b)

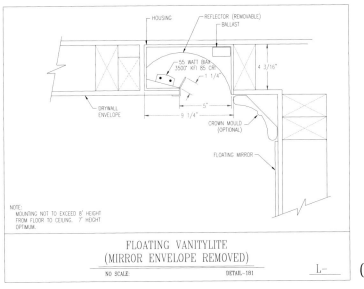

(c)

Figure 15.2
This vanity area has all of the elements that make a master suite sweet. Comfortable and artistic with the addition of decorative wall sconces, low-voltage art accent lights, and the task Vanitylight ™ for full face and body illumination. (The addition of the reading lamp near the chair edge was added after the project's completion and is a hazard due to its proximity to the bath tub).
(Karen and Richard Gomez Residence)
(Photographer: Andrew M. Mitchell, FPI)

Figure 15.3
This ski resort home's guest bath adds sparkle through the low-voltage accent lights that illuminate the etched glass behind the tub. (reflected in the vanity mirror). In addition to the wall sconces, adjustable accent lighting over the vanity and area downlights add to the lighting effects.
(Photographer: Andrew M. Mitchell, FPI)

Figure 15.4
Indirect lighting on top of the vanity soffit gives a nice glow to this elegant master bathroom. Decorative candlestick lamps flank the sit down make-up mirror and low-voltage downlights and wall sconces add to the lighting at the vanity itself. Additional recessed downlights in the high ceiling give adequate area lighting when needed. (Photographer: Mary E. Nichols)

Figure 15.5
This traditional vanity area is dramatic as well as functional. With low-voltage accent and area lighting, decorative sconces and make-up table lamps create a warm and inviting environment. (Photographer: Mary E. Nichols)

Figure 15.6
This private salon boasts custom linear lighting designed by the lighting designer behind the etched hinging mirror. The end result is full face and body illumination for hairdressing, make-up, and general grooming. In addition to the specific task lighting system, a decorative hanging fixture adds to the traditional setting and general ceiling lighting adds to the ambiance of space.
(Photographer: Andrew M. Mitchell, FPI)

Figure 15.7
This heavy paneled vanity area is a tribute to fine wood crafting. The lighting for this space is two fold. Vanitylighting ™ recessed in the bottom soffit of the cabinetry gives the viewer excellent make-up, shaving and general grooming with a balance of decorative wall sconces that add to the period style of the cabinet. Simple and effective.
(Photographer: Andrew M. Mitchell, FPI)

Figure 15.8
Clean and refined, without the
typical bozo bars. There is
nothing more distracting than
bar lights attached to the mirror
with softball size light globes.
Recessed Vanitylighting ™ adds
the appropriate illumination for
the recipient with general ceiling
lighting adding to the space.
(Dan and Kim Huish Residence)
(Photographer:
Andrew M. Mitchell, FPI)

Figure 15.9
This refined powder room is
intended be a sophisticated
extension of the entry and family
areas. This is an excellent
example of style as opposed to
grooming function. Strip lighting
added under the glass sink adds
a sparkling effect. Art accent
lighting and decorative sconces
are all this space calls for and
sure to be a conversation piece.
(Karen and Richard
Gomez Residence)
(Photographer:
Andrew M. Mitchell, FPI)

CHAPTER SIXTEEN:

Cabinetry and Bookcase Illumination Techniques

Coordination for cabinetry and bookcase illumination can be difficult. This is primarily due to the fact that what is drawn on the architectural plans often differs from the product delivered to the job site. Clear communication is recommended with the team member responsible for the products' outcome. This will ensure that the appropriate fasciae and other requirements are added to conceal the proposed lighting fixtures.

The lighting requirements for cabinets and bookcases are:
T-8 - ultra light to control dmg.
- Moderate lighting levels for display
- Adequate design of units to conceal the lighting source
- Specification of low heat producing lighting products
- Incorporation into the lighting control system
- Control of ultra-violet output to preserve artwork

Figure 16.1
Potential details for
cabinetry and bookcase
illumination techniques:
(a) low-voltage recessed interior
cabinet lighting,
(b) interior cabinet lighting,
(c) display case fiber
optic lighting,
(d) downlights in cabinet
fiber optic lighting,
(e) under cabinet lighting,
(f) wardrobe lighting,
(g) top / under cabinet lighting,
(h) low-voltage lighting under
bar and counter top.

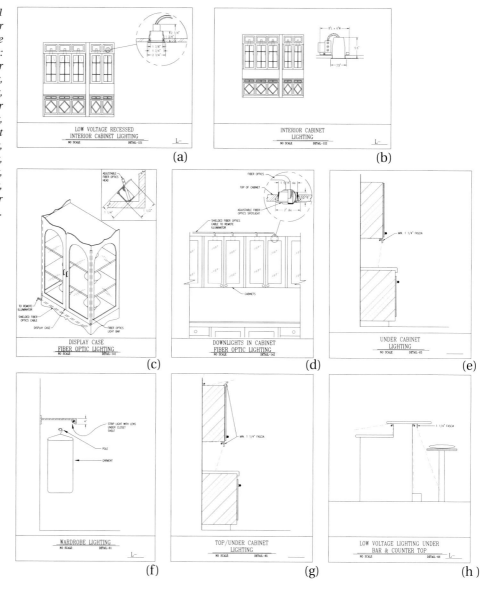

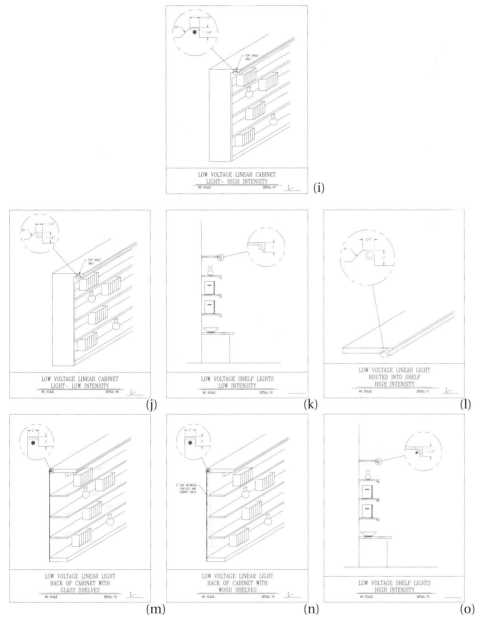

Figure 16.2
Potential details for cabinetry and bookcase illumination techniques continued:
(i) linear cabinet lighting, high intensity,
(j) linear cabinet lighting, low intensity,
(k) shelf lights, low intensity,
(l) linear lighting routed into shelf, high intensity
(m) linear lighting, back of cabinet with glass shelves,
(n) linear lighting, back of cabinet with wood shelves
(o) shelf lights, high intensity.

Figure 16.3
Potential details for cabinetry
and bookcase illumination
techniques continued:
(p) fluorescent uplight,
remote transformer,
(q) fluorescent uplight,
integral transformer,
(r) low-voltage cove lighting.

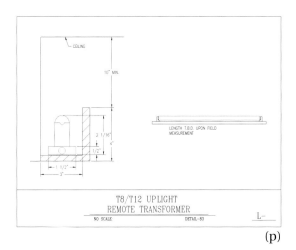

(p)

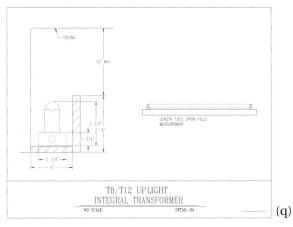

(q)

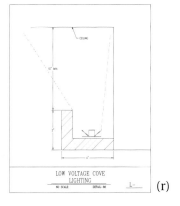

(r)

Figure 16.4
This wine room tasting area had an added twist: wine bottle displays projecting from the stone walls. The lighting designer suggested adding uplighting and downlighting to the display shelves. Details were developed and the metal frame was covered with the same stone veneer. (At the time of this photo, wine bottles were not available). In addition, low-voltage accent lighting highlights the tasting table and leather faced cabinet housing the wine glasses. (Photographer: Andrew M. Mitchell, FPI)

Figure 16.5
This den/media room included cabinetry that the lighting designer detailed in under shelf lighting to highlight the contents. This is an excellent display wall which adds drama and dimension to the room. (Karen and Richard Gomez Residence) (Photographer: Andrew M. Mitchell, FPI)

Figure 16.6
Interior cabinet lighting adds to
this narrow hallway. Well
planned lighting really does
make the difference.
(Karen and Richard
Gomez Residence)
(Photographer:
Andrew M. Mitchell, FPI)

T-13's

Figure 16.7
This wine cabinet display wall is
a woodworking masterpiece.
Interior cabinet lighting, under
counter task lighting, and accent
lighting highlight the
craftsmanship.
(Photographer: Mary E. Nichols)

CHAPTER SEVENTEEN:

Artwork Illumination Techniques

Illuminating artwork is an art in its own right. Residential art may include paintings, sculptures, tapestries, animal collections, automobile collections, and antique furniture. Years of experience and commiserating with curators are the only teachers in this endeavor. The following are a few rules of thumb and examples to point the lighting designer in the right direction.

Guidelines for artwork illumination:
- Learn the limits of the specified lighting products' adjustability
- Be precise in placing the lighting products for the optimum viewing of the piece
- Review the distance charts for low-voltage accent lights and optical framing projectors
- Control of ultra-violet and heat output to preserve artwork, select filters if necessary
- Never try to illuminate a space solely by illuminating the artwork
- Be sensitive to glare off glass or high sheen surfaces
- Never over-illuminate the artwork. Intensity tends to lose dimension
- Try to conceal the lighting products so they do not distract from the artwork
- Add art scene buttons on the lighting control system for drama
- Lighting should be planned with flexibility for artwork rearrangements
- Provide enough wattage capacity in the lighting system and fixtures to re-lamp for increased intensities on certain darker mediums
- The art lighting products should be on separate switch legs or control circuits

Figure 17.1
Potential details for artwork
illumination techniques:
(a) optical framing projector,
top access,
(b) optical framing projector,
bottom access,
(c) MR16 adjustable accent light
with 4 honeycomb louver,
(d) MR16 pin hole downlight
with 4 honeycomb louver,
(e) MR16 light with slot aperture,
(f) Mr16 adjustable accent light
(g) recessed mirror accent light
in sloped ceiling.

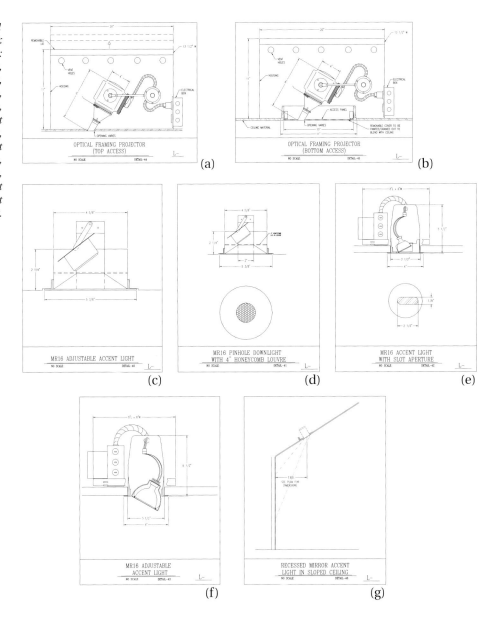

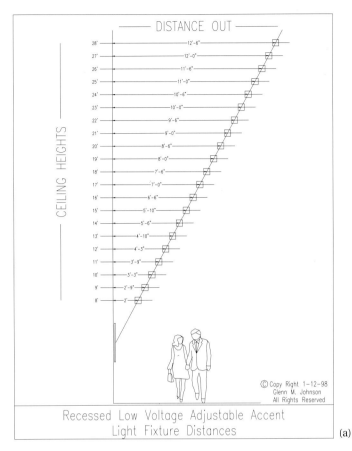

(a)

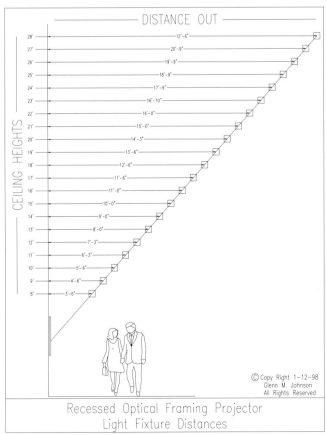

(b)

Figure 17.2
Distance charts for:
(a) recessed low-voltage
adjustable accent light fixtures,
(b) recessed optical framing
projector light fixtures. These
distance charts were develop by
the author to aid in the
placement of recessed accent and
precision optical framing
projectors. Not understanding
these dimensions and the degree
of adjustability for the given
fixture has led to many a sleep-
less night for the inexperienced
practitioner.

Figure 17.3
This graphic depiction is an eye opening example of what happens when the distances are not correct for the application. This 9' ceiling and 40 degree adjustable low-voltage fixture shows the actual light projected and its adjustable limits.

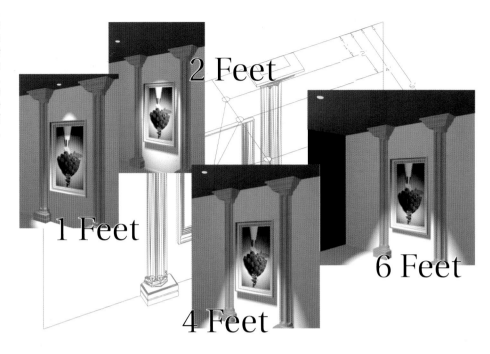

Figure 17.4
This bust is illuminated by an optical framing projector approximately 18' away in distance. In addition low-voltage accent lighting back lights the piece and the double door beyond.
(Photographer: Andrew M. Mitchell, FPI)

Figure 17.5
Sculptural drama is also created by illumination. Low-voltage accents highlight the front of this piece creating dimension with an exciting illuminated backdrop. (Photographer: Andrew M. Mitchell, FPI)

Figure 17.6
The focal point painting over the fireplace is illuminated with an optical framing projector precisely confining the light to the canvas only. In addition low-voltage accent lighting grazes the bookcase. (Photographer: Grey Crawford)

Figure 17.7
This Rocky Mountain home's art
gallery comes to life through
concealed low-voltage
accent lighting.
(Photographer:
Andrew M. Mitchell, FPI)

Figure 17.8
The architecture, muted wall
and carpet colors are only a
backdrop to this colorful art
collection. The lighting designer's
directions from the owner were
simple: make our artwork stand
on its own. Using low-voltage art
accent lighting and dramatic
pools of path lighting the viewer
is guided through a
personal tour.
(Photographer:
Chawla Photography)

Figure 17.9
 You can run but you can't hide in this living room. All eyes are being illuminated by a precision optical framing projector.
(Photographer: John White)

Figure 17.10
 A precision optical framing projector cuts to the core of this metal sculpture.
(Photographer: Merlin Johnson)

CHAPTER EIGHTEEN

Exterior Illumination Techniques

Exterior illumination covers all areas that fall outside of the home's interior envelope. The exterior design team has many of the same members as the interior team. The exterior design team consists of the following design team members and their respective disciplines.

THE EXTERIOR DESIGN TEAM
- The Architect
- The Interior Designer
- The Landscape Architect
- The Soils Consultant
- The Lighting Designer
- The Landscape Contractor
- The Pool Contractor
- The Irrigation Contractor

The Architect

The role of the architect is usually limited to the exterior design and finish of the building and some related hard scape items. Hard scape items might include stairs, decks, patios, planters, or driveways. The hard scape areas are coordinated with the landscape architect.

The Interior Designer

Depending on the scope of the interior designer's service, he or she may be involved in building color selection, window design approval, roof tile recommendations and any decorative lighting placed on the building. All of these processes are coordinated with the architect and lighting designer.

The Landscape Architect

The landscape architect is responsible for the overall site design including contouring, grades, elevations and drainage. He or she is also responsible for hard scape items in the gardens such as pathways, planters, curbing, barbecue areas, gazebos, art or sculpture placement, pool location, spa location, ponds and other water features. He or she also designs accessories to create drama for the grounds by adding tree locations, planting materials, flower beds, and borders. The landscape architect coordinates lighting effects with the lighting designer that will best suit the overall design of the grounds.

It is very important to include the landscape architect in the initial team meeting as discussed in Chapter One. In this meeting, concepts are discussed and budgets are determined for the formulation and ultimate execution of the plans. During the construction process of the home, the excitement and focus is usually concentrated on the house itself and all of the intricate details. The exterior design and landscape concepts come well after the completed roof, the installed windows, and the paint-ready drywall. Unfortunately, once the focus turns to the exterior and grounds, some projects do not have adequate budget preparation and the grounds remain unfinished for a period of time.

The Soils Consultant

The soils consultant plays a critical part in this design team and the success of the landscape architect's work. He or she ensures that the soil is correct for the specified planting and that the selected materials will thrive in the environment.

The Lighting Designer

It is best that the interior lighting designer also designs the exterior lighting design. This procedure will aid in the coordination of the lighting control system that services the interior and exterior space. It also ensures that the design intent remains consistent between the two areas.

The Landscape Contractor

The landscape contractor is the general contractor of the earth. He or she ensures that the landscape architect's wishes are being met in a cost effective and efficient manner.

The Pool Contractor

The pool contractor builds all of the water features as designed by the landscape architect.

The Irrigation Contractor

The irrigation contractor works with the landscape architect in designing and installing all the sprinkler and drip systems for proper lawn, plant and tree maintenance. He or she is also responsible for a water drainage plan. This contractor coordinates with the landscape architect and the landscape contractor to determine the volume and intervals of irrigation system operations.

EXTERIOR ILLUMINATION TECHNIQUES

Exterior illumination often gives the first impression of the home and it should be approached in the same manner as the interior illumination. The philosophy of "hidden is better" also holds true for exterior lighting. The same dramatic effects can be achieved with a lot more flexibility in exterior areas. Exterior areas to be illuminated include:

Exterior Facade
Eaves
Security
Gardens
Pathways
Driveways
Exterior architectural elements
Columns, arbors, gazebos
Stairs
Swimming pools and spa
Fountains, reflecting ponds
Sculptural elements
Hazards to walking and driving

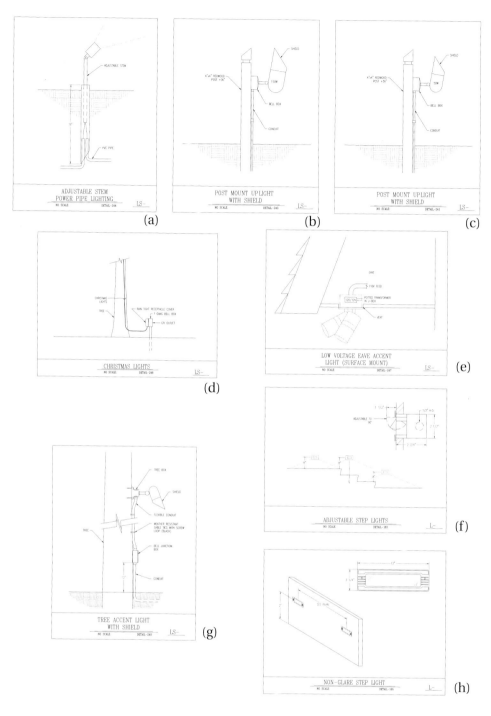

Figure 18.1
Potential details for exterior
illumination techniques:
(a) adjustable stem power pipe
lighting, (b) post mount uplight
with shield, 150 watt,
(c) post mount uplight with
shield, 50 watt,
(d) Christmas lights,
(e) eave accent light, surface
mount, (f) adjustable step lights
(g) tree accent light with shield,
(h) non-glare step light.

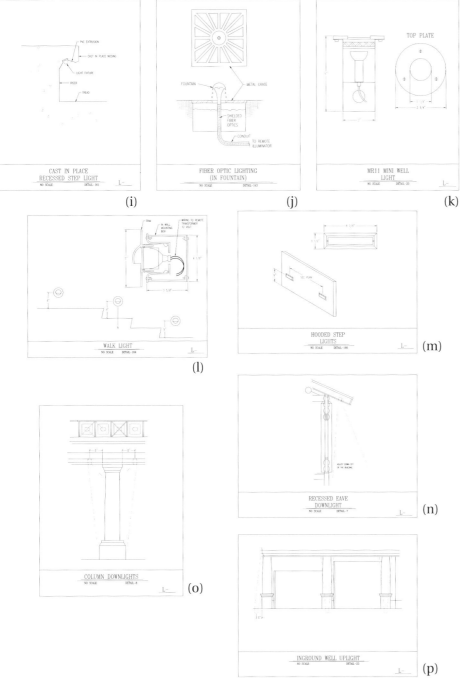

Figure 18.2
Potential details for exterior illumination techniques continued: (i) cast in place recessed step light, (j) fiber optic lighting in fountain, (k) MR11 mini-well light (l) walk light, (m) hooded step light, (n) recessed eave downlight (o) column downlights, (p) in-ground well uplight.

Figure 18.3
This is an example of a
landscape lighting plan.

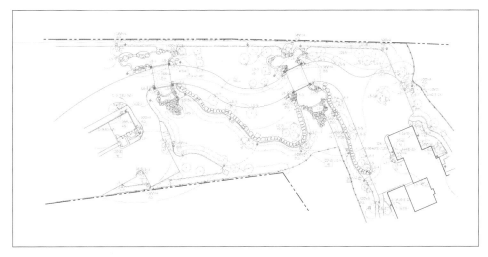

Figure 18.4
Day shot of landscape/ hard
scape sculptural placement with
recessed well lighting.
(Photographer:
Andrew M. Mitchell, FPI)

Figure 18.5
Night shot of the landscape/ hard scape sculptural placement with recessed well lighting dramatically displaying the piece. Low-voltage exterior fixtures uplight the trees in the background adding for a colorful backdrop. (Photographer: Andrew M. Mitchell, FPI)

Figure 18.6
Illumination placed
strategically from a tree accents
the sculpture standing as a
sentinel to the terrace.
(Photographer:
Andrew M. Mitchell, FPI)

Figure 18.7
Tree uplighting recessed in
the lawn and above grade
hedge and path lighting adds to
the focal point sculpture
illuminated from the large tree.
(Photographer:
Andrew M. Mitchell, FPI)

Figure 18.8
Dramatic low-voltage exterior lighting accents foliage, trees and stair from hidden sources.
(Photographer:
Andrew M. Mitchell, FPI)

Figure 18.9
Custom building arch lights designed by the lighting designer adds a breathtaking backdrop to trees, path and exterior sculpture.
(Photographer:
Andrew M. Mitchell, FPI)

Figure 18.10
This elegant setting is a
architectural masterpiece in
the day time.
(Photographer:
Andrew M. Mitchell, FPI)

Figure 18.11
And a glorious multi-
dimensional garden paradise
brought to life by in-pool
lighting, silhouette lighting of the
trellis and path lighting.
(Photographer:
Andrew M. Mitchell, FPI)

Figure 18.12
This home pops out of the desert with subtle illumination that accents the roof top from a location 12 feet in the date palm tree. Low-voltage exterior path lighting, sculptural light and above grade tree uplighting add to this desert experience.
(Photographer: Arthur Coleman)

Figure 18.13
This exterior veranda is as comfortable in the evening as it is in the afternoon. Low-voltage accent lighting and area downlighting warm up the night setting. Note the exterior barbecue light.
(Photographer:
Andrew M. Mitchell, FPI)

Figure 18.14
Strategically placed low-voltage column downlighting and path lighting add to the beauty of this gazebo. Background tree uplighting also adds dimension to this wonderful setting. (Photographer: Randall Michelson Photography)

Figure 18.15
This rustic Rocky Mountain home glows with anticipation as the guests arrive. Strategically placed low-voltage eave lighting creates the drama. (Photographer: Andrew M. Mitchell, FPI)

Figure 18.16
 The fairy tale begins as you
approach this wonderful cottage.
Above grade uplighting nestled
in the flower beds creates the
wonderful foreground effects.
In addition, twinkle lighting
accents a tree near the entry and
tree downlighting adds color to
the beds and patio.
(Photographer:
Andrew M. Mitchell, FPI)

Part 5

Home Trends

CHAPTER NINETEEN

Home Integration;
Home Theater; Home Office

A Holistic Convergence

Homeowners today are quickly becoming familiar with the benefits of exciting products and technologies such as modems, big-screen televisions, or well-designed lighting systems. From the 1980s through the mid-1990s, these and other new products began to pop up intermittently in the homes of a few "early adopters" of new consumer technologies, often hooked together haphazardly.

The old approach to piecing this equipment together had the unfortunate effect of creating clutter and operational confusion, and did little to create synergy among the various pieces. All that is changing. Today, architects, builders, and homeowners are learning an important lesson from a new class of electronics specialist, the Residential Systems Integrator (RSI). An RSI takes a holistic approach to electronics products and services. The RSI's philosophy is that the true power of technology lies not in the individual pieces of equipment, but in the comprehensive integration of all the home's electronic products and services in a way that makes them easy to operate together and maximizes their usefulness to the home's occupants.

In time to support this trend, new product designs are being developed to make integration easier. Manufacturers and service providers are working to take technology categories that once seemed unrelated, such as television and computers, and provide ways that allow them to converge. RSIs, such as Digital Interiors in San Jose, California, are experts in the use and interconnectivity of these technologies, providing the consulting and installation skills to allow homeowners to take advantage of this convergence.

The Language and Reason Behind Integration

The shift toward holistic integration of electronics in the home began quietly several years ago, and has already worked its way into the words we use to describe trends in the home. For example, working or telecommuting from a "home office" is one of the fastest-growing movements across the country. The phrase "home office" describes a concept that obviously refers to the integration of products such as computers, printers, fax machines, multi-line telephones, modems, and Internet access. Ultimately, the power of the home office is dependent on the level of productivity its equipment allows, and the greater the level of integration between all the individual equipment and services used, the more productive the home office can be.

A highly productive home office, therefore, will be one where computers and resources such as printers are interconnected with a wide-bandwidth local area network (LAN), where high-speed Internet service allows independently efficient connections to email, remote servers, and enables videoconferencing when necessary, and where other functions within the home such as security, lighting, energy use, and communications are easily accessible from the computer screen (when necessary) without having to interrupt the work flow. The efficiencies are so high in such a productive environment that work is done quickly and effectively, leaving more time for family and leisure. It is the thoughtful pre-planning and integration of products and services that enables this kind of productive environment.

"Home theater" is another popular trend that uses the language of integration. More kinds of entertainment products are available to us today than ever before. Digital satellites provide high-definition audio, video, even instant Internet access; high-definition digital video disc and laser disc players provide top-quality movie material on big-screen TVs'; surround sound systems with subwoofers exceed the audio experience found in grand movie theaters; and CD players, AM/FM tuners, video-on-demand, WebTV, cable modems, and a host of other services, sources, and fun equipment can create a lifestyle-enhancing variety of family entertainment and background music environments.

But be careful! Patched together without careful planning, all of this incredible equipment can become a nightmare to access and operate, its incredible benefits replaced by headaches and buyer's remorse. Again, the equipment itself is not what is most important. Rather, the proper integration of the equipment into one seamless, easy-to-use "home theater" is the stroke that makes all the difference.

In addition to home offices and home theaters, major electronic subsystems that can be integrated today in the home include multi-room audio/video, telecommunications and intercom systems, lighting controls, satellite feeds, security systems, HVAC equipment, and water management systems.

The Role of Wires

Critical to today's integration of any residential subsystems is the wiring within the home. Radio frequency technologies are developing significantly and may someday get to the point that wireless, high-speed voice, video and data transmission is reliable and consistently accessible. But today, high-speed computer networking and Internet access requires fast wires to pass the data, such as Category 5 (or higher) twisted pairs. Streaming digital or analog video and audio signals from satellite dishes, cable TV feeds, and in-home sources requires well-shielded, wide-bandwidth cables, typically quad-shielded, low-loss, 75-ohm copper-core coax. Dual multi-mode fiber optic cables are an important consideration to ensure ultimate adaptability to future applications. The distribution of this wiring throughout the home, and even the delicate terminations of these cables at wall outlets, should be done by certified technicians to meet IEEE and TIA standards used in the commercial world where many of the high-data-rate technologies were developed. Such attention to the quality of installation and performance of the in-home network is important to ensure that the wires properly support the equipment connected to them.

Access to all products and services, delivery of voice, data, and data at high speeds, and integration/control of the environment should be available to the home's occupant from every important room. For this reason, RSIs such as Digital Interiors suggest installing a minimum of an ultra-wide bandwidth dual coax, dual Category 5 cable bundle from a central distribution panel (called a "star topology") to all bedrooms, family and living rooms, and office areas within the house. These multi-function cabling bundles appear at "Universal Outlets" on the wall, and include AC power from a standard electrical outlet. The power of these "Universal Outlet" locations is that they are flexible enough to support whatever  audio, video, computer, data, telephone, or other equipment the home's occupants choose to use in the room, and allow a single convenient point for plugging all the wires in the wall. The distribution panel, often built unobtrusively into a wall closet, provides a central location from which all cables in the home can be accessed for service, routing, signal filtering, and amplification (if necessary).

Standard "Old home " infrastructure wiring includes:

- Standard 110 volt house wiring as noted in the lighting and power plans
- Standard telephone wiring
- Standard coaxial cabling for television
- Standard security system pre-wire

Today's new technology, infrastructure wiring should include:

- Standard 110 volt house wiring as noted in the lighting and power plans
- Category 5 wiring for voice (telephone),video (video conferencing) and data (PC networking, fax, modem, Internet)
- RG-6 75 Ohm coaxial cable for video (CATV), digital satellite (DSS), camera (CCTV)
- Lighting control wiring determined by the selected system
- Speaker wiring for home theater and background music systems
- Integration wiring to link all systems
- Control wiring for security, intercom, sound, sensors, thermostats, smart cards
- Fiber optic cabling for future-proofing the home

Coax/Category 5 cable bundles should also be run from the central distribution panel to certain areas on the home's exterior. One cable can go to an outside point near the front door to enable camera and intercom communication with visitors. Another should connect the distribution panel the cable TV company and telephone company's hookup boxes at the side of the house (sometimes called "demarcation" points). A third set should run to a properly located site for a satellite dish, on a high exterior wall or on the roof. Additionally, Category 5 multi-pair wires should be run to areas such as the kitchen and bathroom walls where telephones alone may be required. A single Category 5 data line can be run to wall thermostat locations in the home, to allow easy integration of the HVAC system. Less expensive security wiring can be used to sensors at points of entry and for occupancy detectors.

With this Digital Age Wiring Infrastructure in place, the house becomes a flexible environment that can accommodate whatever lifestyle and productivity needs the home's occupants desire, and total integration of all subsystems, whatever they are and wherever they are located, can be achieved.

The following is an example of what can be expected in current and future technology:

Convenience - At the touch of one button, multiple tasks can be executed simultaneously. For example, in the home theater, one button dims the lights, closes the drapes, drops the movie screen, turns all of the electronics on, sets them to the correct mode, and adjusts the volume to create the perfect setting to watch a movie. Remote controls that come with televisions can turn fans and lights on or off. Cellular phones can tell the Jacuzzi to heat up prior to the user's arrival.

Security -An integrated system provides multiple levels of security beyond a simple alarm system. It would allow the home owner to see whoever is at the front door from any television in the house, communicate with them using the telephone, and let them in using the phone. Also, arming the security system can ensure that all of the appliances and lights in the house are turned off and the thermostats are set back.

Entertainment - An integrated system can make the home a much more pleasurable place to spend leisure time. Music can be played throughout the house with the ability to control it from any room. A movie that was started in the family room could be finished in the bedroom without removing the tape.

Conservation - A significant attribute to integration is energy and water conservation. An intelligent home system can adjust fans according to the temperature or if the windows are open. Water management systems can realize if rain has fallen, and adjust the sprinkler schedule.

The Future of Integration

As we grow into the new millennium, the new convergence of electronic products and services will continue. Major corporations are driving the adoption of protocols and standards that will enhance the ability for different products to communicate intelligently with each other. We are very close to a time where the products in our homes will work together to save us money on our utility bills by automatically conserving energy, save us time in ways like reducing the amount of junk mail and "spam" (junk email) we receive by learning what we don't like, and enhance our security by identifying visitors and dangerous situations. Our homes will soon help us to enjoy our leisure time by automatically making available to us the kinds of entertainment and opportunities we prefer, and even enhance our productivity and education by keeping us up to date on important events, appointments, and news that affects our work and our family's development. It's a great time to be alive and experience these incredible benefits of technology, and to recognize that integration, the science that brings the technologies together, is the power that makes it all possible.

Electronic architects command premium fees for design, programming and installation — but, considering provided value, their services are worth the additional cost. The electronic architect coordinates all the sub-systems, cleans up wall device clutter, and combines all the home's functions into one device.

It is also important to remember that wire and its installation is relatively inexpensive. Fees can be budgeted for wiring design and installation. Components can be added as allowed by the budget and a practical approach.

Homeowners should not be fooled by the claims of the audio/video salesman or the electrical contractor when it comes to electronic architecture. These individual disciplines have their place but the above issues should be tackled only by an expert.

Technology has fundamentally changed the way we work, entertain, and educate our children. As thousands of products are introduced to make life more convenient and comfortable, using them becomes increasingly confusing and complicated. Home theater equipment, home office products, and lighting controls can become cumbersome and complicated when neglected. Integrating technology into your home takes careful planning, design, and infrastructure. Most of all, it takes the expertise of a residential systems integrator to do it right.

Glossary of Terms

A Lamp

This lamp is the common light bulb and it is available in clear, frosted and colored finishes.

Accent Lighting

Directional lighting to emphasize a particular object or to draw attention to a part of the field of view.

A.D.A.P.T.I.V.E. Method™

A method developed by the author that walks the designer step by step through the lighting layout. Each letter in A.D.A.P.T.I.V.E. represents a specific area of the design process to focus on.

Ambient Lighting

General illumination.

Ballast

An auxiliary device used with fluorescent lamps to provide the necessary starting voltage and to limit the current during operation.

Beam Spread

The spread of direct illumination from a lamp. The edges of the beam are normally designated as points where the light intensity is half that of the beam's center.

Color Rendering

The effect of a particular light source on the visual appearance of colored surfaces, usually judged by comparison with daylight. A lamp may be assigned a certain color-rending index (CRI) which rates the lamp's ability to render colors. The higher the CRI (based on a 0-100 scale), the better colors appear.

Compact Fluorescent

The general term applied to families of smaller diameter fluorescent lamps (E.g. T4, T5), some of which have built-in ballasts and medium screw bases for easy replacement of incandescent lamps.

Control Station/Keypad

A device that allows an operator to use the computer controlled lighting system.

Control System

A system that allows the control of the balance of lighting in a room or to adjust the levels of light for a specific task or condition.

Decorative Fixtures

Light fixtures used to provide ambient lighting in areas where their appearance contributes to the overall design of the space.

Dimmer

A device used to control the intensity of light emitted by a luminaire by controlling the voltage or current available to it.

Distributed Processing Control System

A system by which several micro-processors are spread throughout the control system and are tied together.

Downlight

Lighting directed downward from luminaires attached to or recessed in the ceiling.

Fascia

Any flat, horizontal or vertical member or molding with little projection.

Fiber Optics

Thin, transparent fibers of glass or plastic that are enclosed by material of a lower index of refraction and that transmit light throughout their length by internal reflections.

Fluorescent Lamps

A high efficiency lamp utilizing an electric discharge through low pressure mercury vapor to produce ultra-violet (UV) energy. The UV excites phosphor materials applied as a thin layer on the inside of a glass tube which makes up the structure of the lamp. The phosphors transform the UV to visible light.

Glare

Any excessively bright source of light that causes discomfort and/or a loss in visibility.

Honeycomb Louvre Lens

A baffle or shielding element constructed in a geometric (honeycomb) pattern to provide shielding from many directions with minimum interference to the desired beam distribution.

IALD

International Association of Lighting Designers

IESNA

Illuminating Engineering Society of North America

Incandescent Lamps

Refers to a light source that radiates visible light from a heated filament (usually tungsten).

Intensity

The amount of light on a particular surface or object.

Indirect Light/Concealed Light

Lighting directed against a reflecting surface, most often a ceiling, to generate diffuse ambient or accent lighting. This light is hidden from normal view.

Linear Strip Lights

A product that has small individual lamps at various spacing along a sometimes flexible molded extrusion with an internal ribbon or standard copper conductor.

Low Voltage Lamp

An incandescent lamp that typically operates at 12 to 24 volts, consuming little energy.

Luminaire

A complete lighting unit consisting of a source or sources together with the parts designed to collect and distribute the light, to position and protect the lamps or sources and to connect them to the power supply.

Lumens

The unit of light by which the output of a lamp is measured.

Luminance Ratios

The ratio between the luminances of any two areas in the visual field.

MR16/11

MR (Multi Reflector) lamp that is a small and powerful 12 or 24 volt lamp. It is often utilized for its excellent beam control.

Motion Controls/Sensors

A sensor mounted in the ceiling or wall that automatically switches the lighting equipment off when spaces are unoccupied or on when they become occupied.

PAR Lamp

(Parabolic Aluminized Reflector Lamp)

PAR lamps have a parabolic shaped reflector. The reflector and lens of these lamps are two separate pieces bonded together. This design yields better control of the beam and the opportunity to develop a number of lens patterns, thus increasing the variety of beam spreads.

Point-By-Point Luminance Calculations

A lighting design procedure for predetermining the illuminance at various locations in lighting installations, by use of luminaire photometric data.

Precision Optical Framing Projectors

A sophisticated lighting device that confines the projected light to a specific object. Through the use of optically engineered condensing and objective lenses in combination with a mask or template the lighting can be precisely confined to the canvas of a painting (not the mat or frame) or to the borders of furniture or sculpture.

R Lamp

Lamps consisting of a one-piece glass bulb with a built in reflector made by applying a layer of aluminum to a portion of the glass. This lamp is not suitable for outdoor applications. Because the coating is applied to a single bulb form, the reflector is not very precise.

Scene Presets

The lighting effect created by adjusting several zones/channels of lighting to the desired intensity.

Transformer

A device that can transfer current from one circuit to another, usually with either a decrease or an increase in voltage. A transformer is an essential component in the installation for any kind of low voltage lamp. There are three types of transformers:

Electronic

Use electronic circuitry. They are small, lightweight and quiet. Their life is shorter than magnetic units.

Magnetic

Use copper wound around a steel core. They are heavy and relatively large. They have a long life expectancy but can produce an audible humming sound.

Torodial

Magnetic (doughnut-shaped) transformer which is quieter than the magnetic transformer but can also produce a hum when controlled by some kinds of electronic dimmers.

Track Lighting

A movable luminaire mounted on a recessed or surface-mounted electrical raceway (track).

Tungsten Halogen

Incandescent light sources utilizing the halogen regenerative cycle to prevent blackening of the lamp envelope during life. Usually more compact and longer life than comparable standard incandescent sources. Also called *quartz, quartz iodine, quartz halogen* or *halogen* types.

Uplight

Any light or light fixture directed in an upward direction.

Vacation Mode

A function of a lighting control system that allows the homeowner to activate pre-set conditions.

Video Conferencing

A method by which involved parties communicate by means of a video connection, through a computer network.

Wattage

A measurement of how much electricity a lamp uses.

Xenon

A small 24 volt lamp that burns very bright and produces a white light, used mainly for cove/indirect lighting applications.

INDEX OF SUBJECTS

INDEX OF LIGHTING DESIGNERS

INDEX OF ARCHITECTS AND INTERIOR DESIGNERS

Resource Appendix

Locating the Author:

Glenn M. Johnson, IALD, IESNA
Principal, Lighting Designer
3945 S. Wasatch Blvd. Box 248
Salt Lake City, UT 84124
e-mail: gmj@spdesign.com
Web site: spdesign.com/resident.html
Services offered: Lighting Design—Instructional Seminars—Business Consulting

Training Seminars and Lighting Labs

IESNA Lighting Education
120 Wall Street
New York, NY 10005
(212) 248-5000 x 115 - Education

IALD
The Merchandise Mart, Suite 487
200 World Trade Center
Chicago, IL 60654
(312) 527-3677

GE Lighting Institute
1-800-255-1200
or (216) 266-9000

Cooper Lighting
THE SOURCE
(847) 956-8400

OSRAM Sylvania
LIGHTmobile
(508) 777-1900

Lightolier
TechCenter
(508) 679-8131

UNIVERSITIES THAT OFFER PROGRAMS IN ARCHITECTURAL LIGHTING DESIGN

Kansas State University, Manhattan, KS
(913) 532-5964

Parsons School of Design, New York, NY
1-800-252-0852

University of Kansas, Lawrence, KS
(913) 864-3434

Pennsylvania State University, University Park, PA
(814) 863-2086

University College London, London, England
(+44) 171-391-1738

University of Colorado, Boulder, CO
(303) 492-4798

Rensselaer Polytechnic Institute, Troy, NY
(518) 276-8717

ADDITIONAL BOOKS TO READ

Creative Lighting: Custom and Decorative Luminaires
Author: Wanda Jankowski
Publisher: PBC International Inc., 1997

Designing with Light: Residential Interiors
Author: Wanda Jankowski
Publisher: P B C International Inc., 1991

Interior Lighting for Designers
Authors: Gary Gordon and James Nuckolls
Publisher: John Wiley & Sons, Inc., 1995

Architectural Residential Lighting
Author: Randall Whitehead
Publisher: Rockport Publishers, Inc., 1993

Radiation Light & Illumination
Author: Louis Erhardt
Publisher: Camarillo Reproduction Center, 1977

*The Lighting Book: A Buyer's Guide to Locating Almost
Every Kind of Lighting Device*
Author: Martin Greif
Publisher: Main Street Pr., 1986

Illumination Engineering
Author: Joseph B. Murdoch
Publisher: Macmillan Publishing Co., 1985

Architectural Lighting Design
Author: Gary Steffy
Publisher: Van Nostrand Reinhold, 1997

The Landscape Lighting Book
Author: Janet Lennox Moyer
Publisher: John Wiley & Sons, 1992

Detailing Light: Integrated Lighting Solutions for Residential and Contract Design
Author: Jean Gorman
Publisher: Whitney Library of Design, 1995

Lighting: In Architecture and Interior Design
Author: Wanda Jankowski
Publisher: Pbc Intl., 1995

Louis I. Kahn: Light and Space
Author: Urs Buttiker
Publisher: Watson-Guptill Publications, 1994

PERIODICALS

Architectural Lighting
Miller Freeman, Inc.
One Penn Plaza
New York, NY 10119-1198

LD+A
Illuminating Engineering Society of North America
120 Wall St.
17th Floor
New York, NY 10005

Architectural Record Lighting
McGraw-Hill, Inc.
1221 Avenue of the Americas
New York, NY 10020

Home Lighting & Accessories
Doctorow Communications, Inc.
P.O. Box 2147
1011 Clifton Ave.
Clifton, NJ 07015

Audio Video Interiors
McMullen Argus Publishing, Inc.
774 S. Placentia Ave.
Placentia, CA 92870-6846